Growing Up Together

Teens Write About Being Parents

By Youth Communication

Edited by Al Desetta

True Stories by Teens

Growing Up Together

EXECUTIVE EDITORS
Keith Hefner and Laura Longhine

CONTRIBUTING EDITORS
Nora McCarthy, Kendra Hurley, Al Desetta, Duffie Cohen,
Andrea Estepa, Sheila Feeney, and Laura Longhine

LAYOUT & DESIGN
Efrain Reyes, Jr. and Jeff Faerber

COVER ART
Edward Cortez and YC Art Dept

For reprint information, please contact Youth Communication.

ISBN 978-1-933939-88-9

Second, Expanded Edition
The first edition of this book was entitled *I'm the Mommy Now.*

Printed in the United States of America

Youth Communication ®
New York, New York
www.youthcomm.org

Table of Contents

Contents

Contents

Introduction

In this book's opening story, the teen writer has sex with J.W., a guy she has just met. J.W. pretends to use protection, but doesn't. The writer becomes pregnant and, in the weeks that follow, a familiar pattern develops. "He blamed me for keeping the baby," she writes. "I blamed him for giving me one."

But that's only the start of the writer's problems. She feels "numb and trapped" because while she doesn't want a baby, neither does she want an abortion. Since her parents never played a major role in her life, the writer is deeply worried about becoming a mother.

"I feel that a child should have both his parents, yet I'm bringing a child into the world who, just like me, will probably miss his father," she writes. "J.W. tricked me into having unprotected sex, but I'm also responsible because I didn't know him."

Yet, despite her anger and fear, the writer decides to have the child and deal with the consequences, "determined to give my baby a better life than I've had."

Raising a child is a difficult experience for parents of any age, but when you're a teenager, the problems can seem overwhelming. In these honest and courageous stories, teen parents don't spare us any of the bad news about having a child at a young age. Yet, at the same time, these young people are facing challenges and growing as individuals as they struggle to provide the nurturing their children need and deserve.

No one can read this book and take lightly the idea of becoming a teen parent. Most of these writers don't have jobs, a high school diploma, or a stable support system. Many are in foster care, such as Lillian Cremedy, who is routinely locked out of her foster home while she's pregnant. After she gives birth, she doesn't find a stable foster home until her fifth try. As Fetima Perkins writes, "A lot of people tell teenage girls not to have babies. I never really listened to anyone who said that to me. But now that I have a baby, I know why adults are always saying it."

But in the end, this is a hopeful book. Some teen fathers who have the urge to run away instead get jobs, pay child support, and learn to parent their children. Shauntay Jones heroically juggles the demands of school and a baby. Fatima Plummer forms a support group with other teen parents. T. Davis gives up behavior that endangers her child. Anzula Richardson, with the help of a mentor's program at a maternity residence, gains strength and sets goals for the future.

As Vanessa Sanchez writes, "Growing up in a negative environment doesn't mean you can't flourish."

But most of all, these writers want young people to learn from their mistakes and not have children before they're ready to provide the kind of support a child needs. As Fetima Perkins points out, "You're going to be the example your child follows, whether you're a good example or not, so do yourself a favor: before you think about having a kid, finish school, go to college, and get a good job. Then have all the kids you want."

In the following stories, names have been changed: *AWOL from Motherhood, Growing into Fatherhood, Mom Wasn't Ready for Me, I Wish I Had Waited,* and *Dates With Destiny.*

Edward Cortez

Mommy's Baby, Daddy's 'Maybe'

By Anonymous

One night last winter I got all dressed up and cute for a night out on the town with my friend Robert. I was waiting downstairs when I saw a guy in a stylish black jacket and dark blue jeans. He was cute and cut, with biceps and a six-pack. Muscles weren't a problem for him.

"You live here, don't you?" he said. He told me his name was J.W.

Just then Robert was pulling up in front of the building in a cab, already drunk. He was three hours late so I decided to ditch him. I just got some Henny off him and showed him the door. J.W. popped, "That was your man, right?"

"No!" I said. As I walked up the stairs, I felt J.W. watching me from behind. He kept asking why I didn't have a man and saying that I knew his mother.

I did know his mother. She often rang the bell to my apartment to get buzzed into the building because J.W. was rarely home. She also buzzed me in when I didn't have the intercom key.

Realizing that J.W. was the son of a lady I knew made me feel like I knew him. And it turned out he lived right down the hall. When he asked if I wanted to come over and watch movies with him, I felt safe.

I admit it: I wouldn't have minded if we kissed a little bit. I was in the mood. I was used to getting it on the regular and hadn't gotten any since I'd dumped my ex-boyfriend a few months back. If sex happened, then it happened.

J.W. tricked me into having unprotected sex, but I'm also responsible because I didn't know him.

J.W. held his door for me. It was dark in his crib. "Don't be scared. I won't bite," he smiled. "Well, not yet."

It was appealing to me to be with a neighbor. I was tired of talking to boys in the streets. Being close to him felt really good. Even his Burberry cologne turned me on. He started asking me questions.

J.W.: "So, where your man at?"

Me: "I don't have one."

J.W.: "Why not? Ain't like you're ugly."

My dad was never really around to teach me the ways of men, so I didn't know that the lines J.W. was laying on me were the lines of a player. I just wanted to get close to someone, to have someone give me the attention I needed. I wanted to forget about my ex and my frustrations and have a guy's attention focused only on me.

When he kissed me, I tasted the Henny we'd been drinking. A smooth vibration sucked me in and I felt mesmerized. The way he made love made me think I must be "the one" for him.

With the liquor in my system (plus a blunt I had smoked while getting ready), my judgment was slightly—OK, fully—impaired. But I saw a condom on the dresser and saw him put it on. I was relieved that I didn't have to ask. At the moment, all that mattered to me were the good feelings.

In the morning, J.W. held me close and said, "I came in you twice last night and I think you might be pregnant."

"J.W., what are you talking about?"

"I'm too young to have a baby," he said. "If you're pregnant, you need to get an abortion."

I felt dazed. "What about the condom you put on?" I asked.

"I took it off while we were having sex," he said. He sounded proud. "I could have lied," he added, as though I should be grateful.

I wanted to cry, but held in my tears.

Why would a guy do such a thing without even telling me? As I sat there stunned, he started screaming, "Look, look! I got my test two weeks ago and see? I'm clean." He pulled out a paper from his top dresser drawer that said he didn't have HIV.

"Thanks for the insight," I thought.

When I left, he told me he would call me later.

I went home and cried, feeling numb and trapped. I didn't want a baby. I wanted to get the morning after pill, but then I thought, "It's Saturday. How could I get it?" (Later, I found out that I could have called Planned Parenthood to get emergency contraception, even on a Saturday, and that you have up to five days after having sex to take the pills.)

I felt dumb for not being able to see that J.W. didn't care about me. I felt I couldn't raise a baby by myself and I started thinking, "If I am pregnant, an abortion sounds excellent. That's exactly what I'll do."

J.W called my house every day. He insisted that I at least find out if I was pregnant.

So exactly a week and a half later I went to the clinic with my heart in my throat and said, "I'm here to take a pregnancy test." The first test came out inconclusive, but the second one came out as clear as day. Two stripes prove you're pregnant and I was.

J.W. kept calling, worrying if I had eaten and asking, "What is your decision going to be?" I kept telling him I didn't know. I was never placed in a position where I had to decide if I wanted something or not. This was a challenge for me.

I thought about scheduling an abortion, but I never did. I just kept blowing it off and delaying. Deep down in my heart I wanted the baby.

Because I'd had a medical problem four years earlier, I thought I might never be able to have a child. I'd never felt real, actual love from another human being. I thought this pregnancy might be my only chance to have a child who could love me. And I felt that caring for this baby would be the first step to becoming a real woman.

My friends couldn't believe I was pregnant and said I was throwing my life away. Everyone wanted to know who the father was, but I didn't tell them.

My grandmother said, "How could you be so stupid and get pregnant when you haven't even finished college? What were you thinking? How come you didn't make him use protection?" After 10 minutes of yelling, I said, "Grandma, I gotta go."

The only two people who really had my back were my uncle and aunt. They said if I needed anything they would help out. Nobody else had much positive to say. It started to dawn on me that I wouldn't have a lot of support raising this baby, but I still wanted it.

I came from a background where parents never played a major part in their children's lives. It was hard growing up because my family was so dysfunctional. We fought all the time and we could never cope with our problems.

My father wasn't there to see me come out of my mother's

womb because he was in the Army. I met him when I was 4 and loved him, but he and my mother divorced when I was 7. My mother's abuse got worse after my father left, and I blamed him for not being there to protect me. By the time I was 10 I hardly saw him.

I invented a rosy image of the family I would create for myself one day—me, a father, and our children. It would be nothing like the family I came from.

Even though I knew it wasn't realistic, I hoped that once J.W. found out I was definitely pregnant he'd become remorseful, expressive, and open-minded. I wanted the father of my child to be there for us.

Since his own father was never around for him, I thought J.W. would understand how important it was to help raise

He blamed me for keeping the baby. I blamed him for giving me one.

his child. I thought that we should both do everything in our power to raise our baby together since neither one of us had stable fathers in our lives.

But he didn't see things that way.

When I asked for his thoughts about planning for our baby, he would just say, "Whatever you want to do, D." I didn't want to make all the decisions because I was afraid he would hold me accountable for mistakes. And I wanted him to show he cared by having an opinion.

Things went bad between us really fast. I tried to be understanding, but every time we talked, we fought. J.W. is stubborn, and so am I. He blamed me for keeping the baby. I blamed him for giving me one.

I got angry that even though J.W. didn't have a job, he couldn't be there at my doctor's appointments to see his own baby on the sonogram. I got concerned that he thought he could just pop in and out of my child's life, just like he popped in and out of mine. I didn't want my child to be hurt.

*E*ventually, I had to realize that J.W. was a rooster and I could not depend on him for anything. The last time we talked, he told me, "Don't be asking me any questions. You ain't my girl and you ain't my father." Then he started calling me names.

A part of me is angry, sad, and scared. I feel that a child should have both his parents, yet I'm bringing a child into the world who, just like me, will probably miss his father. J.W. tricked me into having unprotected sex, but I'm also responsible because I didn't know him.

Another part of me doesn't want to give up on J.W. I don't want my family to say that I'm just like my mother, who could never make her relationships work out. And, of course, I'd like my baby to have a father. It's hard to give up that rosy image.

Still, I'm happy about becoming a mother and determined to give my baby a better life than I've had. I hoped that the father of my child would be around, but I realize that with all our fights and miscommunication, this may not happen. While J.W. figures out whether he's going to step up, I'm making plans of my own.

I'm at a home for unwed mothers right now and I'm exploring a move to Atlanta, upstate New York, or New Jersey. I want to finish college and get a degree in criminal science or radiology. I might not be able to give my baby a reliable father, but I can at least keep my promise to myself that no child of mine will have to worry about where his next meal is coming from.

I know that J.W. is frustrated and young. Maybe he'll grow up and become responsible. But I also realize that's something I can't count on. For now, I have to accept that this child is my baby, but J.W.'s "maybe."

The author was in high school when she wrote this story.

Leo Maisouradze

AWOL from Motherhood

By Shannel Walker

When I got pregnant at 14, some of my family members told me that I was too young to be a mother. My uncle said, "All of y'all kids wanna open your legs, and now y'all making babies and y'all don't have no jobs."

Then my aunt came out of her mouth saying, "You know you are too young. Your party days are over."

At the time I felt scared and unprepared. My boyfriend had broken up with me. I had no money. Becoming a mom was not my plan. Still, their comments made me mad. How could they talk about me when most of them had kids at age 14 or 15? I told myself, "I don't care what they say, I'm having my baby."

But two months after I gave birth to my daughter, Marvia, I went into foster care. My grandmother, who I lived with, put me in a group home for two years. Once I got there, I saw what my family meant about teen moms. Some girls did try to grow up and act like good moms to their kids, but it seemed like nine times out of 10 the teen mothers I met were not ready to become moms.

One friend, Tasha, didn't seem ready to be a mother at all. I met Tasha three months after I got to the group home and we both liked to joke around. We would chill and show each other's kids some attention.

Tasha had two kids—a 3-year-old named Britney and a 1-year-old named Jordin—and I got real close to them because they were always coming in my room to play with Marvia. We would sing and play hand games. I'd even put them to bed some nights.

When Tasha spent time with her kids, she and the kids had a good time. But usually she acted lazy about her kids. She totally ignored them when she was on the phone, talking for hours before she'd bother to change her son's dirty diaper.

The way she ignored her kids made me mad. I remembered how much it hurt when my father ignored me.

And she did not want to listen to anyone. If the staff told her to change Jordin's diaper, she'd say, "Leave me the hell alone, I know when my son is wet." People were always telling her what to do, but she didn't want to hear it. She was only worried about herself and no one could change that.

Tasha was mad that the group home was really strict. Even though she was 18, she didn't have the freedom to hang out all night and be stuck up on some guy.

Most days Tasha said she was going to school, but would actually meet up with a boy, then come in mad late or stay out until the next day. Tasha thought that she could party first and then spend time with her kids when she wanted to.

The way she ignored her kids made me mad. I remembered how much it hurt when my father ignored me. I knew how her kids felt, but no matter what I said Tasha didn't want to change.

Tasha had a long history of ignoring her kids. When Britney was a few months old, Tasha had been charged with neglect. Britney had gone to live with a foster family for almost two years.

Tasha knew how hard it was to grow up in the system—she'd been in care since age 8. Tasha eventually got Britney back, but I guess she still didn't feel like putting her kids first—after she'd been at our group home for a year, she went AWOL and left her kids behind.

One Sunday around 6 o'clock, after I had just come in from a home visit, a girl told me, "Tasha has been AWOL since Saturday and left the kids here."

I thought, "What a selfish fool. She has two beautiful children and all she can think about is being with some guy?"

All the girls and the staff thought it was one more game she was playing, so the staff didn't call the cops to report her right away. As the days went by, I helped staff take care of Britney and Jordin. I noticed that the kids didn't even ask where their mommy was. But Tasha went AWOL a lot, so I guess her kids were used to it.

After a few days, her son's father called looking for her. He said that he was going to call the cops. Soon the cops came and spoke to the staff.

When I walked into the office, I saw one staff crying. My heart dropped into my stomach. I knew Tasha's children were going into care. The two kids I loved like my own son and daughter were leaving me.

In Tasha's room, the staff members were packing the kids' clothes.

"Is there anything I can do?" I asked.

"Can you take Britney's hair out and clean her up?" they asked me.

As I took Britney out of the bathtub and dressed her, she started to cry. I thought, "She knows she's leaving. All I can do is hold her one good time." Then I started to do her hair and, as I did each braid, I felt as if she was moving farther away from me.

Everyone came outside and crowded around the van when it was time for the kids to go. Jordin was calm, but Britney was still crying.

I went inside, looked at Marvia, and thanked the Lord that it had not happened to me. Marvia said, "Jordin, Britney." I didn't know what to say. I couldn't believe that Tasha would leave her kids for a guy.

In a way, it was also for the best. The kids needed more love and attention than the fake love Tasha was giving them. But who knows if they will find that love in the system? I wish Tasha had thought about the kind of future her kids might have growing up in care.

I grew up because I wanted to give my daughter a better childhood than the one I had.

When I saw how Tasha refused to grow up, I could understand why adults tell teenagers not to have babies while they're young. Being a mother is a rough road—I know that now from raising Marvia. I do think the best bet is to wait to have a baby until you are stable and on your own.

When I had Marvia I felt really motivated to change, so I could show my daughter and my family that I could be a good mom. Even though I didn't like the group home, I tried to make my stay better by joining anything I could. I joined the Youth Council, which planned group home activites, and got an award for volunteering in the community.

But if I didn't know I'd eventually be going back to my grandmother's, I think I would have bugged out in the group home. That place was strict and there was always drama between the mothers. It would have been hard to keep from feeling trapped, like I was stuck with a life I couldn't control until I turned 21.

Maybe that's how Tasha felt, but I don't know. I don't understand why Tasha left her kids. I don't know if she has anyone in her life who really cares about her or not.

But I think the biggest difference between us is that she didn't want to be a mom. The only way to be a good mom is to love your children and put them first. I grew up when I had Marvia, because I wanted to give my daughter a better childhood than the one I had. Tasha didn't. She treated her kids like little dolls she could play with and then put back on the shelf.

Shannel was 19 when she wrote this story.

Jolie Prom

Weaving Our Own Safety Net

By Fatima Plummer

When I was 19, I became pregnant with my daughter Mia. I was terrified. The foster care system barely took care of me. I wondered how I would take care of both of us.

At the time, I was living with my fiancé's family. Because I was an undocumented immigrant, the family court judge had required that my agency hold me in care until I turned 21, even though I went AWOL to my boyfriend's house. My caseworker allowed me to stay there because I was being responsible and not getting into any drama.

But when I got pregnant, my caseworker thought I should move to a mother-child program. If I did, my fiancé would only be able to visit once a week. To me, that was a big problem. I believed my daughter should see her father every day. Otherwise, how could she bond with him? Children need their fathers as much as they need their mothers.

I lost my own father because he was murdered when I was 3 years old. Even though I never met him, I've always missed having a dad. I hope that he and my grandfather look down on me from heaven.

My fiancé and his father were close. Before his father died, they went out to family dinners and Little League games. I wanted my daughter to have that kind of relationship with her father. So my fiancé and I decided that I would continue living with him.

I remember sitting in a half-lit room, telling my caseworker that I was not going to a mother-child home. She kept saying, "You're making the wrong decision." She thought I was thinking only of myself, not my daughter, and warned me that my fiancé wouldn't be there for me all the time. (She was wrong. Three years later, we still live together and have a great relationship.)

The day I went into labor I was so scared. I don't remember, but my fiancé says that my mood was off the wall when we got to the hospital. I was cussing out the nurse whenever I felt the contractions. He tells this story all the time.

I believed my daughter should see her father every day. Otherwise, how could she bond with him?

Once I gave birth, my fiancé and I felt so much joy we cried. When the nurses weighed Mia, my fiancé would not move from her side. At one point they had to take Mia out the room and he wanted to go too. I was amazed by how much we loved this little person that we'd just met.

Still, those first few weeks were exhausting and frustrating. I'd believed Mia would sleep through the night, but she woke up if there was any noise in the house. We couldn't turn on the TV or radio, and still she woke up all the time.

I also didn't realize how expensive babies are. I asked my caseworker for financial help when the Pampers started running out. She said that the foster care system would give me a stipend for Pampers and milk, but it never came. I was furious that the people who called themselves my guardians wouldn't give me the help I needed. My fiancé and I were on our own.

Luckily, my doctor told me about the national WIC program, which helps new mothers pay for infant formula, milk, cheese, eggs, and cereal to provide the fiber, calcium, and vitamins children need to develop and grow strong. WIC also gives parenting classes. I felt good the first day I went. Everyone was nice, and some of them were pregnant or had small kids themselves, so they knew what we were going through.

I thought only young mothers would come to the WIC classes, but when I came in the door I noticed that there were more older moms than young moms. I realized then that it's never too late to ask for help. Raising a child at any age is difficult. I learned a lot in that class, like when to start the baby on solid foods and how to keep from overfeeding her.

My fiancé was already working and as Mia got older, I found a job, too. I asked my case manager for help finding a babysitter. She told me that I could get ACD, a babysitting program run by New York's foster care system.

At first, I loved the program. It found me a great babysitter named Ana. I felt safe leaving my daughter with her because she always had activities for the kids. Mia was not just sitting around, she was learning.

Soon I got a flyer telling parents that all ACD clients must attend parenting classes or lose their babysitting services. The first day I came straight from work to the class at an agency in my neighborhood. There was a big table with juice, coffee, snacks, and booklets for the parents. Because the neighborhood is mostly Dominican, all of the booklets were in Spanish.

Well, I am Latina, but I never learned to read Spanish. When I asked for a booklet in English, they didn't have any. One lady even said, "You should know how to read Spanish, or you are not Dominican." I felt like kicking the daylights out of her!

Then the teacher started teaching the class in Spanish. I didn't understand everything she said, so I raised my hand and asked her to translate for my fiancé and me.

"You are Spanish," she said. "You should understand."

"Yes, I am of Spanish descent," I told her. "However, I don't understand some of the words you're using."

"You're stopping the class from learning. I'll find the information for you in English and mail it to you," she promised.

I felt I was sitting there just for show. I started thinking to myself, "For all this, I could have gone home and spent some time with my family."

The English booklet never came. When I asked for it at the next class, the teacher said, "You'll have to deal with what we have."

I felt very angry. My fiancé and I were trying to learn about raising our daughter, but it seemed like the agency that was supposed to help us only cared about getting paid. After that, I decided I'd be better off learning to parent on my own.

So my fiancé and I decided to build our own support system. We formed a support group with four of our older friends who already had kids. We all called each other when we needed advice. One friend in particular, Christine, helped me a lot.

I asked my caseworker for financial help when the Pampers started running out.

On bad days, I would tell her, "I'm feeling so depressed and overwhelmed!" She would give me the keys to her apartment and let me stay there the whole day. Christine had a beautiful antique tub. She'd tell me, "Use my sea salts and get in the bath." Being in her apartment, which was clean and quiet, relaxed me.

I also joined Voices of Youth (VOY), an advocacy organization for youth in the foster care system in New York City. At VOY, I became a pubic speaker and learned to train child welfare professionals to be sensitive to teens' perspectives. I also learned that it's easier to learn from peers who support each other than from an expert.

The VOY staff, who have all been in foster care, taught me to get my point across without cursing or getting violent. When my fiancé and I had disagreements over the best way to raise our child, we used to get upset with each other because neither one of us felt like we were heard and understood. I learned not to get into it at the moment, but to say, "Let's talk about this later." Then, after the baby was in bed and it was quiet in the house, we'd talk.

What helped the most was buying a parenting book, which offered information and advice about a baby's stages from birth to age five. At first, when Mia was not feeling well, my fiancé and I would go crazy. We read the book to find out what to do.

My fiancé and I decided to build our own support system.

One time Mia had a rash. I was going bananas until my fiancé and I looked in the book together. Her symptoms sounded just like eczema. The book listed questions to ask the doctor, so when we took our daughter to her check-up we were prepared. Luckily, it wasn't a bad case. We just had to apply some hydrocortisone cream.

Another time my daughter was crying and pulling at her ear. I looked in the book's index and found that she probably had an ear infection and I had to call the doctor. When I was feeling the most nervous as a mother, the book helped us ask the simple questions that allowed us to get the right answers.

Mia is now 3 years old. I still learn something new every day about being a parent. But our friends, my work at VOY, and the book allowed me to calm myself down a little bit. I believe that my fiancé and I are doing the right things to instill in her a positive frame of mind.

I'm so glad that my fiancé and I are raising our daughter together, and I'm sure that we made the right decision. My daughter and her father have a very different relationship than the one she has with me.

When she's hurt or sad, Mia wants to be with me. When she wants to run wild and play, she goes to her daddy. With me, she gets in trouble. With her daddy she can do no wrong. If he does get mad, she always listens. "Didn't your mother tell you to stop?" he'll say. "OK, Da Da," she says, and she'll stop right away.

Looking back, I wish that the foster care system had support groups for mothers and fathers. Along with financial help or a roof over their heads, new moms and dads both need help learning to parent their children.

Fatima was 22 when she wrote this story. She attended college and earned a degree in computer information systems.

YC Art Dept.

Growing Into Fatherhood

By Julio A. Pagan

Starting when I was about 12, I began thinking about having a son, someone I could play with and teach my strange and crazy philosophy.

I was always good with my little cousins and nephews. I would play with them and they'd laugh. I would read them stories I'd written and take them to the park so they could learn how to play football. It felt good having them around and I knew I wanted a child of my own some day. But I never expected to have one at such an early age.

I was 16 and a junior in high school when I met Maria. She was 15 and a freshman. I was playing the drums for a band in church and she would send me little notes with my sister. I thought this was childish but I liked it.

We started going out. Sometimes, she would sleep over at my

house after attending night services at our church in Manhattan because it was too late for her to travel back to Brooklyn alone. She usually bunked with my sister.

One night, about a month into our relationship, Maria stayed over on a really hot night. I had a fan in my room and my sister didn't. It was about 2 o'clock in the morning when she walked into my room to ask if I would lend her the fan. I asked why, if all she had to do was sleep in my room. After 30 minutes of persuasion, she agreed. And that night it happened—we made love.

Two months later, during the month of May, she told me she was pregnant. Other girls have told me that just to get my reaction, so at first I thought she was playing around. Then I noticed her eyes were watery and that she had this serious look on her face. When I finally came to my senses, I began to think: what about school, what about my job, what about me?

Actually, I was not as worried about her being pregnant as I was about telling my parents. My father had his first child when he was 17, and always warned me not to make the same mistake. He explained to me that having a child when you're young causes problems, like having to get a job and having to drop out of school.

The same thing happened to my cousin, who had his first child when he was in his senior year in high school and never graduated.

My father had his first child when he was 17, and always warned me not to make the same mistake.

After that he had six other children and he never got a GED or went to college. My father told me that if it happened to me, I would have to face it on my own.

An abortion was out of the question because I didn't have much money and I didn't know about places that offered free services. When I told Maria, she started to cry as if her life was over. I admit I really thought mine was too. But we talked and came to a decision.

She would have the baby and I would help her in any way I could. While she was pregnant I would travel to Brooklyn every other day to visit her. After the baby was born, I would take care of it during the week so she could go to school and she would have him on the weekends.

We did it that way because I was closer to graduation and I knew I would find a way to finish. I didn't want to be responsible for Maria messing up her life like my cousin did. After she graduated, she would take the baby during the week and I would be the one to see him on weekends.

After a couple of days, we talked all this over with our parents. Our mothers were surprised but not angry. But when my father found out, all hell broke loose. He explained to me how I would not be able to stay in the house any longer. How the trust he had for me was gone and how it would take a long time for it to be regained.

How would my son feel if his father didn't graduate from high school or didn't go to college?

When Maria's stepfather found out, he was even angrier than my father was. But since he's in jail, there really wasn't anything he could do about it.

During the months Maria was pregnant, our relationship got a little rocky. We would argue almost all the time. I would tell her not to smoke but she would anyway. Or we would argue for no reason at all. We started seeing and talking to each other less and less every month. I think our relationship just wore out. It got to the point where she didn't even want me around her.

Even though we weren't together, I still wanted her to have the child. My feelings for the baby didn't change, I guess, and neither did my feelings for Maria.

The night she went into labor, we were in church. It was about 9 p.m. and my parents rushed her to Lincoln Hospital in the Bronx.

That night was the most paranoid night of my life. All the feelings I held inside since the day she told me exploded. I used the bathroom at least five times. All sorts of things went through my mind. Is it going to be a boy or a girl? Is it going to be deformed? And, a question I didn't enjoy asking myself—is my child going to die? I was worried about that because my grandmother's first child died shortly after its birth.

I always saw myself as a strong person but this was too much to handle. I didn't go into the delivery room simply because I couldn't. Maria had been angry at me the whole time and I guess I couldn't handle all that pressure. Her mother went in instead of me.

The first time I saw the baby, it didn't feel like he was mine. It felt just like the times when I used to go to the hospital to see my cousin's children. I didn't feel like a father.

It's been a year and a couple of months now since Israel's birth (it was my mother's idea to give him a Biblical name). Maria kept the baby with her for the first five months to establish a motherly relationship. She knew she wasn't going to see him much after he came to live with me.

I've moved out of my parent's house (my father wasn't kidding about wanting me to deal with this on my own) and during the week Israel stays with me. Most of the time my grandmother takes care of him while I'm at work or school. There are times when Maria comes over to stay for a while when she has a fight with her parents, but that doesn't happen too often.

I usually spend about two hours with Israel in the morning and five when I come home from work. When I get home he is usually in his stroller raising hell with my grandmother. I quickly take him out before he starts crying (something he always does when I come home to get me to pay attention to him). We'll play with a collection of different balls I've gotten for him or I'll sit him down in front of the window so he can see the kids play outside. I always bring him a bag of Cheese Doodles (his favorite food) and I enjoy watching as he wolfs them down.

At times I feel I don't spend enough time with him but I can't. I was in my senior year when he was born, and I had to work and miss school a lot so I didn't graduate. Now I'm working hard so I can graduate in June. I plan to enter college next fall. If I don't sacrifice a couple of hours with him now and finish school, I feel as if he isn't going to have a good financial life when he grows up. How would my son feel if his father didn't graduate from high school or didn't go to college? What kind of example would I be?

Right now, Maria only sees Israel on the weekends. I don't think he realizes that she's his mother—he thinks my grandmother is. I do admit I won't feel like a true father myself until I'm older. Right now, I'm more like a big brother to him. But I am trying to teach him how to grow up strong and how to not take life too seriously all the time.

Since the time Maria and I separated I've often thought about her moving in with me permanently, but I guess it will take a long time before we can be a real family. I worry about what's going to happen when Israel moves back in with her. I've gotten used to seeing him every day, watching him dance when the radio's on or seeing him drive my grandmother crazy by throwing stuff to her and then running away. I don't ever want to be just a weekend father.

Julio was 18 when he wrote this story. He later earned a degree in criminal justice at John Jay College.

Phillip Rollano

Mom Wasn't Ready for Me

By Anonymous

My mom was only 16 when she had me, her first child. By the time she was 23, she had three little girls. I don't think she was ready for any of us. She needed more time to deal with the problems she had while growing up. She didn't need the lives of three young girls adding to her own issues. But she went ahead and had us before she was ready. Now, partly because of all this, I'm in foster care.

If I'm not mistaken, my mom told me she had me so young because she wanted someone to love and to love her back. I understand the need to be loved, but if you want someone to love you, get a dog. Once you train that dog to love you, it knows nothing else. But a baby's not like that. A baby doesn't just give like that. A baby takes and takes and takes and takes. If you have a baby because you want to receive love, you're bound to be disappointed and the baby will feel it.

I don't think my mom realized any of that. I don't think she realized how difficult it is to be a mom while you're still trying to grow up yourself. So she went ahead and had us. She hopped and skipped right over her childhood, and then she stumbled. And we, her kids, struggled with her.

By the time I was about 8, I already had too much responsibility. My mom supported our family financially, but she had me supporting us in other ways. It's like she was the working wife and I was the housewife.

After school I would come home and do my homework, make sure my room was clean, and help my sister with her homework. Then, after the other kids were asleep, I was still up doing my chores. I'd clean the dishes, scrub the bathroom, and iron my baby sisters' school clothes. I would also get my grown mama's clothes ready for her to wear to work the next day. And on the weekends, I washed everyone's laundry.

Now, I don't mind helping my mom out around the house, but that's just too much. I feel like I missed my childhood trying to clean up after my family. But I didn't feel like I could say no, because if someone wasn't doing all the things I was doing at home, I might have gotten put into foster care much earlier than I did.

So now I have strong feelings about teen pregnancy. I think people should wait to grow up before they have babies. If you wait, you have more time to learn how to deal with stress without resorting to violence or neglect. You also have time to save money for a child and get used to holding down a job. You'll be less likely to blame your children for opportunities you might miss out on.

Having babies at a young age can make everyone in the family struggle more than they need to, especially the kids.

So when I attended a conference on urban girls (which I thought should have been named "Ghetto Girls"), I looked forward to hearing the part about teen pregnancy. I thought that some of the speakers might be teen moms themselves, and some might have been the daughters of teen mothers, like me. I figured we'd all talk about teen pregnancy and how it had affected our lives.

That wasn't what happened. Instead, everyone who went to the session on teen motherhood sat around listening to adults tell us about the teen moms they had interviewed. (Why couldn't those moms have just talked for themselves?) But what surprised me the most was not that adults were doing all the talking, but that they talked only about the teen moms, and not about the children of teen moms. Some of them talked about how it was nonsense that teen moms can't succeed in life. One spoke about a teen mom who, several years after having a child, was actually more successful in her career than her sister, who had not been a teen mom.

Well, it's obvious that a teen mother can still become whatever she wants in life. Of course teen moms can finish high school and work good jobs. My mom has a good job, and I'm proud of her for it. But what about the children of teen mothers? Will those kids get the love, care, and attention they need while their teen parents are busy trying to grow up and be successful?

I don't think my mother realized how difficult it is to be a mom while you're still trying to grow up yourself.

Not once during the session did I hear anyone ask a question like this. Not once did I hear anyone talk about what can happen to the child of someone who isn't ready to be a parent.

I know too many teen mothers who act the same way after they have a child as they did before they had a child. In my agency some teen mothers walk around in name brand clothes, while their children's clothes are raggedy and don't fit. It's clear to me that those moms care more for themselves than they care for their children.

I once knew a teen named Shauna. She was the perfect description of an unfit mother. Shauna had two jobs—one that paid and one that didn't. Unfortunately, Shauna only took the paid job seriously. She gave only the slightest bit of time to her other job—being a mother.

Shauna would wake up and get ready for the job that paid her. Then she'd come home that evening to the job she didn't really care for. If only she knew that her job at home was the most important job!

Shauna's precious little life at home, a 4-year-old boy named Leo, rarely got the care he needed. Shauna was hardly ever home to give him motherly affection. When she was home, she didn't want to be bothered with him. She was succeeding in the world, but she was neglecting her son. And what will happen to Leo as a result? Will he be able to grow up strong after not getting the attention he needs?

Some teen mothers walk around in name brand clothes, while their children's clothes are raggedy and don't fit.

The National Campaign to Prevent Teen Pregnancy says it will be a hard path for him. According to their 1997 study "Whatever Happened to Childhood?: The Problem of Teen Pregnancy in the United States," children of teen mothers tend to have more difficult lives than kids born to older parents. Children of teen mothers do much worse in school than those born to older parents, and they are much more likely to repeat a grade. Children of teen moms also have a higher rate of behavior problems. They suffer higher rates of abuse and neglect, and are more likely to go into foster care, like I did.

But the problems don't end in childhood. Young adult children of teen moms are much more likely to be neither working nor going to school. The sons of teen mothers are 13% more likely to end up in prisons. Daughters of teen moms are 22% more likely to become teen mothers themselves. (Which won't happen to me!) Of course, teen moms tend to be poorer than other moms, and a lot of these bad outcomes stem more from poverty than the fact that the mom is a teen. But there's no denying that if you're poor and you become a parent, your kids will have a steeper hill to climb in life.

So how could anyone, in good conscience, conduct a workshop on teen pregnancy and spend the whole time talking about how a teen mom can still finish school and succeed? When a child is born, that's one extra person that must be saved in this hard world. So thinking about the mother first is not something I tend to do. The first thing I think about is getting her child the love and care it needs. Why do so few people think like this?

We need to ask tough questions when talking about teen pregnancy: will the teen mother make sure that child is well protected? Is she financially able to raise a child? Has she had a chance to learn how to handle stress in healthy ways? Or will she abuse or neglect that child?

My own mom truly loved me and wanted the best for me. She did not want me to grow up like she did. She wanted me to have things that she didn't have, and she wanted me to live a better life than she lived. The only problem is that she wanted it too soon. She had me before she was ready, and ended up giving me the same hard life she had.

The writer was in high school when she wrote this story.

Elena Hawley

There's More Than One Way to Be a Father

By Frank Marino

Shortly before Christmas I got a call from Daquan, a friend from my old high school in Brooklyn. Back when we used to chill together, Daquan was a regular, irresponsible teenager—careless and always cutting out of school. But now it was like I was talking to a totally different person. Since the last time we spoke, Daquan's life had changed tremendously.

Last year, his girlfriend Joanne got pregnant. They decided to stay together and raise their child the right way. But shortly after the baby was born, a disaster changed everything: Joanne was hit by a car and killed. This left Daquan, who is 19, to raise the child on his own.

Although he admits that it's an enormous responsibility, Daquan says he doesn't regret becoming a father. "I wouldn't change it for the world," he says, adding that the baby is "the only special thing in my life."

In the year and a half since I'd seen him last, Daquan has gone from hanging out with friends and being free, to becoming a committed and responsible parent. He told me it was a hard adjustment, but he never had a father around to raise him, and he doesn't want his kid to grow up that way.

"It's very hard, but I just try and think positive and do the best I can," Daquan said. "Sure, I get worn out and tired, but I just keep pushing myself, and telling myself 'Daquan, you have to do it, be strong.' "

Daquan is different than other teenage fathers I know. Many teen fathers I've spoken to—including guys I'm friendly with—have the wrong outlook on parenting. They think having a child is a big joke, like it's a hobby to make babies. Some just keep on hanging out with their buddies, leaving the mothers to depend on welfare checks and look after the children without any help.

For example, my friend Sam, who is 18, doesn't spend much time with his child. For Sam, being a teen father is a drag. He hates having to be responsible for a baby.

Daquan has gone from hanging out with friends to becoming a committed and responsible parent.

"You lose your freedom," Sam complained. "Life changes tremendously. I thought having a kid was a piece of cake—you feed him, change him, and that's it. Then you get doctor's bills and food bills, and clothing also adds up to a lot of money."

To find out what it's like to be a teen father who really accepts the responsibility of raising a child, I decided to spend some time with Daquan and his son, Eric, who is seven months old.

Daquan has no family or girlfriend to help him, and he takes parenting seriously. Just before Eric was born, Daquan got a good steady job at a beer distributing company. He makes about $300 a week, enough to support himself and Eric.

Daquan rents a room in a friend's house, where he and his baby share a bedroom. His friend's parents watch the baby while he works. "I come home every day at 6 o'clock and spend the rest of the day with him. Saturday night is the only time I really hang out," says Daquan.

When I went to visit Daquan on Christmas, I began to understand what it's like to be a teenager raising a baby all alone. On holidays I'm used to relaxing with my family and eating all the delicious food my grandmothers cook. But for Daquan it's very different. Since he doesn't get along with his own family and his friend's parents are the closest thing to family he has, he shared their holiday dinner.

Even so, Daquan wasn't relaxing and hanging out. He was busy in the kitchen heating applesauce, and patiently cleaning what Eric splashed all over himself and his seat. Afterwards Daquan calmly gave him a bottle and changed his diaper. He was never careless and never let Eric out of his sight, always making sure he didn't get hurt playing.

He never had a father around to raise him, and he doesn't want his kid to grow up that way.

"Wow," I was saying to myself. "Imagine if that was me. I would be pulling my hair out right now." But Daquan kept his cool and never lost his patience, and even told me that he was enjoying Christmas with his baby.

Besides visiting Daquan, I interviewed other teen fathers who are trying to take responsibility. I went to a program for teen fathers at a YWCA in Manhattan where I met some guys who, in spite of a lot of obstacles, were really trying.

Talking to some of the guys in the program made me realize how hard it is for a teen father to raise a young child while trying to finish school, work, and do anything else. One participant, Tyquone, 17, had to drop out of school and get his GED when he became the father of a baby girl a year and a half ago.

"It's a hard responsibility because my girlfriend has to work and pay for the expenses," said Tyquone. "I have to stay home and watch the baby. I also look for jobs, but it's real hard out there."

Hearing what their lives are like made me realize that there are teen fathers out there who don't fit the negative stereotype. Listening to them, I thought to myself, "Here are guys who really don't have much in life, but they still manage to be there for their child." Some of them told me that they owe a lot of their positive attitude to the coordinator of the program, John Gomez.

When I spoke to Gomez, he told me that the program "helps teenage fathers get more involved in their child's upbringing." Many of the guys he sees are overcoming major obstacles besides parenthood. He estimates that 80% are high school dropouts and 20% have no fathers themselves. Adding to their troubles, he says, are the financial demands involved with raising a baby.

"The most difficult problem for teenage fathers is they feel they are looked at by their girlfriends as wallets," said Gomez. My friend Sam seems to agree with that. Sam says he hates being tied to the baby's mother, who he'd been with less than a year before the baby's birth.

"I went from being free to being a human robot," Sam said. "All I hear is 'Give me money.' " He feels that his obligation to the baby is forcing him to stay in the relationship. "It's like we just hold on for the baby's sake," Sam says.

The teen fathers' program helps people like Sam get their lives on track and become better parents. "We make them become responsible and more motivated and interested in their child," Gomez said. He told me that they help many of the guys by finding them jobs, so they can provide for their families.

I always thought most teen fathers today felt like Sam. I was relieved to see that there are good, caring fathers out there. Talking to Daquan and the fathers from the program at the Y really opened my eyes and made me realize that teen dads can do the right thing. Maybe with more programs like the one John Gomez runs, more young fathers would be like Daquan or Tyquone.

Frank was 18 when he wrote this story.

Elizabeth Deegan

I Wish I Had Waited

By Fetima Perkins

There's a poster in my school that says: "A baby costs $471 a month. How much do you have in your pocket?"

Good question, huh? I think all teenagers should have that poster on the ceiling over their beds, so they get a reminder every time they lie down. (That was several years ago. I'm sure the cost has gone up since then.)

A lot of people tell teenage girls not to have babies. I never really listened to anyone who said that to me. But now that I have a baby, I know why adults are always saying it.

A year ago, when I first realized I was pregnant, my attitude was like, "So what? I don't care. I wanted a baby."

I hoped I could hide it from my mother as long as possible and not get kicked out of the house. More importantly, I hoped that I'd have a healthy pregnancy and become a good mother. And keep my job.

Too bad that's not what happened.

I guess I wanted a baby because I knew I had a lot of love to give to someone and I'd always given it to the wrong people. I figured if I had a baby, I'd be able to give my love to someone who deserved it and would appreciate it, and most of all, someone who needed it.

I also wanted to be able to be a better mom than my mother, to be more understanding, and be able to have my daughter talk to me about anything. I wanted to be a friend to my child.

Now I wish I saw all of the responsibilities coming. I wish I saw that I would be taking care of the baby mainly by myself, depending on people to get her everything, and then having my dependency thrown in my face.

Like a lot of girls, I thought my boyfriend would be there to help me and financially support me. But like most girls, I quickly found out that this was not going to happen.

I wish I saw that I would be taking care of the baby mainly by myself.

When I told my boyfriend at the time, Alex, that I was three months pregnant, he hit me and tried to kick me, so needless to say, things with us weren't exactly going to work out. (And since then it's gotten worse—I had to take out a restraining order against him.)

When I realized he wasn't going to act like a father, I felt like a fool. The first question that popped into my mind was, "What made me think he was different?" I felt so stupid.

Then again, I was also glad, because I figured I don't need a nut case around to teach Destiny the wrong things in life.

Later I realized I didn't even like him as a boyfriend, and I felt good and hurt at the same time. I felt good because I was glad I got out of that relationship before I became another story on the 10 o'clock news and Destiny was gone before she got here.

But I was hurt and still am hurt because he was the first person I could talk to. He understood exactly what I was going through, not "uh-huh-ing" me to death.

Alex made me feel special and was extremely romantic when he was in his right mind, and part of him is a beautiful, big-hearted person. I guess it hurts everyone to lose a good friend.

Plus, after Alex and I broke up, I realized I had no one to depend on. And when I lost my job (by the end of my pregnancy I couldn't work as a cashier all day), I didn't have any money, either.

Many girls think they're going to get on welfare when they get pregnant, but I'm here to let you know, I don't think so! They've changed the rules, and it's a lot harder to get the government to support you.

Unless you're 21, living on your own, or homeless, forget about it. And don't think going to these places and sitting in those uncomfortable chairs for hours while you're pregnant is a piece of cake, because it's not.

Sure, you can get food stamps, WIC, and Medicaid, which are easy to get if you're pregnant, but that's not enough money for the baby's crib, diapers, clothes, toys, blankets, bottles, and everything else you're going to need.

I have to get my mom or my current boyfriend Tony (not the baby's father) to pay for those things.

But money worries are only part of the problem. As a new mother, you learn a lot very quickly. Like how to grow up—that's forced on you, because your childhood is over.

At 14, or even 18, you're still just a kid. You should be out going to the movies with guys or going to the mall with your girlfriends.

But if you have a baby, you can't do that without bringing your child with you. That's when motherhood kicks you in the gut.

Motherhood takes all your time and love. As far as fun goes, at first you can forget about it. The only fun you'll have is with your baby, because you're not going anywhere except to the kitchen to make a bottle and back to the baby's room.

Don't get me wrong. Being a mother isn't all bad. There are some good things about it, too, but it takes a while to realize that. In the beginning, you think you're going to lose your mind.

And having my baby has not only made my own life more difficult, it's also put a lot of stress on my relationships with my family and friends.

Having a baby has affected my relationship with my mother in many different ways, mostly bad. When she gets upset, she likes to remind me that she is the one buying things for Destiny and that I have no money for anything, so I need to watch what I say or else I'll get nothing from her.

She's also always telling me things about Destiny like I'm stupid, instead of saying them as a suggestion.

I thought my boyfriend would be there to help me and financially support me.

And things with my boyfriend got more complicated, too. After I broke up with Alex, the baby's father, I got back together with my previous boyfriend, Tony, who I had been with for two years before that.

Actually, at one point we both thought Tony was her father, but one day I was watching a movie at Tony's house and I just knew that Destiny was Alex's.

I wrote Tony a letter while he was sleeping and told him what happened. I left it by his pillow and kissed him on his forehead while crying my eyes out.

Then he woke up and read the letter and said he had a feeling, and then he held me while I cried on him and apologized repeatedly.

At the time, Tony wasn't sure about how he felt about being a father to Destiny, but eventually he said that it wasn't the baby's fault that she had a messed up father.

By then, he had gotten attached to her and she to him (it seemed like she could recognize his voice, because she would always kick me when he put his face to my stomach).

The thing that really made Tony fall in love with her is when we went for a sonogram and found out her ear was against my stomach so she could hear him talk.

I've been really impressed with how serious Tony is about being a daddy.

But having Destiny has also caused a lot of arguments between us. He's supposed to watch her on certain days, and sometimes he'll say he's on his way and then never show up. Then I get in trouble because my mother has something to do but she can't do it because she has to babysit Destiny.

Besides, all the problems between Alex and me have made Tony hate Alex even more. If I mention his name Tony gets very upset, which is understandable.

A while ago I took Alex to court for child support and soon after that he came to my house and was threatening my daughter and me and trying to kick the door down. Now I have an order of protection against him, but his violence still scares me, and every time I have to see him in court I get upset.

Alex was her father, but he's not her daddy.

It's also stressful that Tony and I don't have any time alone just to talk. I don't even remember the last time he and I went out by ourselves.

Maybe the reason why a lot of young girls think having a baby is fun is because a lot of parents tend to take care of their children's children. So, every time a girl sees her friend, even if she knows the friend has a baby, she never sees her with the baby. Her friend is always going out and partying. I feel that any parent who takes care of her kid's kid is downright stupid!

Having a baby is no joke, and parents who allow a child to leave her baby with them are basically telling their daughter: go back and have another baby!

Don't get me wrong. Every mother needs some time to herself every once in a while. And my mother definitely helps me watch

Destiny. But most of the time I'm just sitting home with her, and I rarely see my friends. I guess the burden of having a baby really hits home when my friends ask me to go somewhere and I can never go.

All this complaining is not to say that I don't love my baby—I do! That's why I am willing to sacrifice so much for her.

But do I wish I had waited to have a child? Absolutely! Sometimes I think, "I'm almost 20 years old, it's club time and time to be hanging out late at night," but I can't do that.

I also wish I'd waited to get a steady job, make enough money to have my own apartment, and not have to depend on anyone.

As a new mother, you learn a lot very quickly because your childhood is over.

I feel if you're not financially ready to have a baby—which basically no teenager is (including myself)—then it's selfish and inconsiderate to bring a baby into the world.

There is nothing wrong with having a baby, but you should want to have enough money and education to give her the best in life and spoil her if you choose to. You should be able to teach your child more than ABCs and 1,2,3s—she deserves that you set a good example.

It was really hard for me to finish high school once Destiny was born. I'm still planning to go to college. I guess I'm not sure how that's going to work out, though.

But how am I going to tell my child to finish school if I don't?

You're going to be the example your child follows, whether you're a good example or not, so do yourself a favor: before you think about having a kid, finish school, go to college, and get a good job. Then have all the kids you want.

See Fetima's story about raising her daughter,
starting on the next page.

Jacob Reinstein

Dates With Destiny

By Fetima Perkins

I'm glad that my boyfriend Tony helps me with the baby. But I'm sick and tired of having to depend on him to get this little girl everything, because having to ask him for stuff is like pulling teeth. I really want a job of my own so that I can buy her what she needs and tell him to keep his money.

I'm really frustrated, and I tend to take my anger out on Tony. But then again, most of the time it's him I'm mad at anyway. Right now it's really hard being a new mother and all, but I guess I'll get used to it eventually. I don't want to be all negative, though.

It seems like everyone always tells you that you'll have pain and suffering (you will), but they don't tell you that being a mother is the greatest thing in the world and they don't tell you how rewarding it is.

There are times when I feel like I'm going to lose my mind,

and there are times when I can't picture my life without Destiny Faith.

I see how she has grown so beautifully since she came home. I love that she knows my voice and the way she looks at me with so much admiration in her eyes, like I'm the world to her.

Right now she is my reason for not going crazy, and most of all she is my reason for wanting to finish school, get my diploma, try to find a job, and go to college.

Even though she is only a few months old, she motivates me to do the right thing and to keep away from the life that I used to lead. I guess in a nutshell what I am trying to say is: she is everything to me, and she is my destiny.

Here's my diary of my days and nights with Destiny in the weeks after she first came home.

October 5

Tony and I took the baby on the bus to K-Mart so we could get Destiny some Pampers and a bottle warmer. We tried to find some newborn Pampers and they didn't have any, so we figured we'd go to the K-Mart at Astor Place, but we checked every pharmacy along the way and none had any newborn Pampers. Eventually we found them at Duane Reade and got them for $7.69, which is too much money for only 28 Pampers.

Tony thought I had been such a good mother that I deserved a night out, so he took me to Uno's. I enjoyed myself because, Lord knows, I needed a night out, but it wasn't really a night out because I had the baby with me.

I had buffalo wings and tried to enjoy them without making a mess and getting sauce on the baby, and I did it. I waited for my dinner forever, and when I got it I enjoyed it. Tony had baby back ribs and he gave me a piece, and I got barbecue sauce on my jeans. The baby got her hands in the sauce and wiped it on my chest, and I didn't know it was there until I looked.

After we ate I fed her a bottle of milk, but after she drank she spit up. I had to try to wipe her up at the table while Tony just sat there.

There are times I get so aggravated because he doesn't do anything and I do everything, and it's hard as hell to do this by myself. Recently Tony spent the night, supposedly to get an idea of what a night with Destiny is like, but when she woke up to get fed he was still sleeping because he sleeps so heavy. So, once again, I was left to feed her all night by myself, even though Tony was there. I was very pissed off and had an attitude when he woke up, because I was tired and he was rested, and that wasn't the agreement.

Destiny is going to be one month next week, and I have not gotten a decent night's rest since she's been home. That's all right because she's worth all my time, but I feel exceptionally tired and aggravated. When I look at her the tiredness goes away, because her beauty lets me know that she's just doing what comes naturally and she doesn't know any better.

I guess I had a better than average day because I got to go out and not sit at home and stare at the four walls.

October 6

We stayed indoors and, I must say, this little girl amazes me every day. The doctor says she's very advanced for her age and she proved that again today. As I was feeding her, she put her hands on the bottle and held it like a big girl. I am very proud of her and I hope she's just as advanced when she gets to school.

Tomorrow we have a big day because we have to go to Elmhurst Hospital so she can get her own WIC benefits for formula and so I can get more WIC benefits for myself. (WIC stands for Women, Infants and Children. It provides benefits to help ensure that children get a good start, even if their parents—like me—can't afford some of the things they need)

We need a bunch of papers to get together so we can get in there and get out, so now that she's asleep I can try to get those papers together.

October 8

I spoke to Tony this afternoon and he said he has no money to buy milk or Pampers for the baby, so now Destiny has no milk and only eight Pampers left.

October 9

It's Friday afternoon, Tony just came over to see the baby, and we just finished arguing about how he acts like he doesn't care about the baby having no Pampers and no milk.

I told him he comes over when it's convenient for him and when he's rested, while I no longer know what rest is. I have to feed her every three hours and burp her and change her and stay in the house and stare at the four walls all day.

He told me I should get over it because it's all a part of being a parent. I told him I don't mind doing it, but don't call me and tell me where he's been and who he's seen because I don't care.

Destiny is going to be one month next week, and I have not gotten a decent night's rest since she's been home.

He doesn't do anything when it comes to the baby except come over, play with her, and stare at her while she's sleeping. Then he goes home and does whatever he pleases.

I basically told Tony that unless he can be here at 8:30 a.m. and deal with her all day, then don't come over at all, because it's time he gets a taste of what it's like having to be with her all day.

Now it's Friday night and I actually left the house alone, to be by myself for the first time in three weeks since she was born.

I didn't have anywhere to go and none of my friends were home, so I walked around the corner in the rain nice and slow and enjoyed every minute of it.

I went out because I was sick of staying in the house and figured since Tony was here it was high time he learns to take care of Destiny by himself, so I left her with him and my mother.

Whatever he needs to know, he can ask my mother.

When I got back, my mother said she thought it was funny that he didn't know what to do when Destiny was crying. I paid her no attention. Tony was still holding her and feeding her when I came in, and she eventually went to sleep.

Then he and I talked and straightened things out and we were hugging and kissing again, because he said that after I left he had time to think, and he understood why I was so upset.

October 10

This morning, while Tony was watching the baby, I took a shower, washed my hair, and played my music. I stayed in there for an hour and enjoyed every minute of it.

I never would have been able to take a shower like that any other time, because the baby would be in her carrier and getting irritable. So you know I'll never forget that shower.

Maybe I'll take another one again someday.

Destiny is going to be four months next Saturday and it seems like I just brought her home the other day. I would never have guessed in a million years that she'd be so advanced.

She stands up already and she's started teething. Every day I look at her and see how beautiful she's become. In a few short months she'll be one year old, not to mention walking and talking, if not in high school already (ha ha).

In the first few weeks after I got her home from the hospital, I thought I was going to lose my mind. I used to cry when she cried, and I'd get upset when my mother told me she's soaking wet just by feeling her diaper. I couldn't feel the difference from a dry diaper, but now I can and I'm damn proud of it. I also never knew what Destiny was crying for, but now I know what's wrong just by the sound of her cry.

I never really started feeling like a mother until just recently, because my grandfather came back from Antigua and has been helping me out financially, giving me $20 a week. A lot of people may say that's no money, especially when you have a baby, but I'm here to tell you, you're wrong. You just have to spend your money wisely.

As far as Tony goes, he and I are doing much better. He understands now what hard work it is being a mother. I am very happy to say we haven't argued in three months straight, and if we sense any tension, we talk about it and resolve it right then.

He now buys Destiny cute little outfits when he sees something he likes, and he'll buy her baby food without me having to ask him. He and I have a good understanding of what the baby needs.

It really feels good to have someone who is helpful by your side. Right now, the hardest thing for him will be trying to make time for the baby while attending college.

She motivates me to do the right thing and to keep away from the life that I used to lead.

Tony won't admit it, but I know he also feels Destiny's grown so quickly that he doesn't even know what's happened. It probably seems even quicker to him than it does to me, since he only sees her when he's not working.

And I think he's scared like I am. Even though we can't wait for her to walk, that will be another whole responsibility, because then we'll have to watch where she's walking off to.

Fetima was 19 when she wrote this story and the previous one.

Ling na Lin

A Day in the Life of a Teen Mom

By Shauntay Jones

5:00 a.m.: The alarm goes off, but it's not any ordinary alarm. This alarm goes off at all different times without warning. The alarm is the sound of a screaming baby—my baby.

At first I ignore the cry, hoping it will die down. But it doesn't, so I sleepily turn over to give my 1-month-old daughter her pacifier. She keeps crying. I'm getting frustrated—in about one and a half hours I'll have to get up and get ready for school. I force myself to get up and go into the kitchen to make her bottle. My daughter is in my arms and still crying.

The bottle bobs in the boiling water. I take it out, checking it on my wrist to see if it's too hot. Luckily, it's just right. I walk back to my bedroom, sit on my bed, and begin feeding my daughter. I stop to burp her after every three ounces she drinks. When she's done, I lay her down and pat her back so she'll fall asleep.

6:30 a.m.: I close my eyes and the alarm goes off. (The real alarm, this time.) Realizing that a whole hour and a half has passed, I bolt straight up. I grab my towel off the nightstand and jump in the shower. As the hot water hits me, I can feel my body weakening. I start to doze off. To stay awake, I stand directly beneath the water, letting the hot flow hit my face. I get out of the shower, dry off, and get dressed.

I take my daughter off her stomach and turn her around so I can take her clothes off. She begins to wake up, but not fully. I get her washcloth and wash her body down. I put clothes on her that make her look so cute.

7:30 a.m.: I've got to hurry so I'm not late getting to the baby-sitter. I strap my daughter into her carrier, which is attached to my upper body. I begin to complain about how much my back is going to hurt by the time I get to the train. As I'm leaving the house, my boyfriend's sister Lineta says, "Stop complaining!"

After experiencing a day in the life of a teen mom, Lineta is even more determined to save her virginity.

"She thinks it's so easy," I say to myself and roll my eyes.

The subway is six blocks away. Each block my back hurts more. I'm on the sixth block when I see the train pulling up. I start running, holding my daughter. At the turnstile I struggle to get my Metrocard to work. Once through, I run up the steps. "Hold the door!" I shout. I'm catching my breath as people offer me their seats.

When I get off at my stop, I have to walk five blocks to the babysitter's house. When I get there, I decide to relax until it's time to go to school. Resting at the kitchen table feels so good.

8:30 a.m.: I kiss my daughter goodbye and walk to school. The school day always goes by smoothly—it feels like a break from my other life as a mom.

2:30 p.m.: When school's over, I run out the front door and walk quickly. to the babysitter's. The sooner I get there, the sooner I can get home and rest.

I pick up my daughter at the babysitter's and walk to the train, which makes me so tired and mad. Sometimes I want to take a cab, but I'd rather not waste money to avoid a walk I know I can do. So I just handle it and keep going.

Once home, I have an hour to rest before I leave and go to night school. This has been my schedule for the last seven months.

But my routine changed one Friday morning. I was on my way out the door, complaining about walking to the train and how heavy my daughter was getting, when my boyfriend's sister Lineta said, "Please, Shauntay, you act like it's hard what you do every day. All you're doing is taking her to the baby sitter, then picking her up and bringing your butt home. That's nothing!"

I couldn't believe she thought my schedule was easy. So I took off the carrier, passed my daughter to Lineta, and said, "OK, since you think it's so easy, take the diaper bag, put the carrier on, and take her to school with you!"

Lineta shrugged her shoulders and said, "No big deal." She called up her school to make sure she could bring her niece with her. While she was on the phone, I told her the rules—she had to walk to and from the train and couldn't take a cab. I also explained what she needed to do in case of an emergency. I told her that if my daughter cried with the pacifier, it meant she's hungry, and if she started to choke, to pat her back softly.

As I walked to the train without my daughter in my arms, I felt so good. I had no back pains and I was able to walk fast. Being without my daughter felt very different.

When I got to school, my advisor Laura said, "Shauntay, you're extra early and you don't look worn out."

"That's because I didn't bring my daughter to the babysitter," I said in an excited voice. "I came straight to school." Laura told me to have a great day off.

All day I was anxious to get home to see how Lineta's day had turned out. Mine was going great. I felt so free, my back was well rested, and my feet didn't hurt.

After school, when I approached the door to my house, I could hear Lineta pacing back and forth. Before I could take a step inside, Lineta put my daughter in my arms.

"Damn," I said, "was she that bad? And what are you doing home so early?"

"Why am I home so early?" Lineta was still pacing. "I'll tell you why! Your daughter is heavy, greedy, and she threw up all over me in school. I had no choice but to come home! Then," Lineta added in a very sarcastic tone, "while I was attempting to walk home from the train, I had to spend money on a cab because of all the weight that I had to carry!"

"Lineta, you cheated," I said. "You were not supposed to take a cab home. You were supposed to handle it like I do and walk your lazy butt home. Also," I said, mimicking her, "stop complaining. All you did was take her to school and bring your butt back home."

"All right," she said. "I now understand where you're coming from when you say that it's not as easy as it looks. From now on, since I'm the one looking in on the situation, I won't comment, or should I say I won't knock it 'til I try it."

True to her word, Lineta no longer makes comments when I complain. Instead, she even tells others that it's not easy being a teen mom. And after experiencing a day in the life of a teen mom, Lineta is even more determined to save her virginity. She says she doesn't want children until she's married and financially stable, so she can take cabs whenever she wants.

Shauntay was 16 when she wrote this story.

Saretta Burkett

Staying with the Hurt

By T. Davis

Soon after my daughter Anasia was born, her father went off to jail for sticking up a man for his money. So I had to convince myself that I was going to be the happiest single parent there ever was.

I told myself that I was going to give my child everything that she needed and wanted. (Being that I was only 17 years old, I had no choice but to think that way.)

I also told myself that I was never going to hit my child, because I didn't want her to experience the same kind of abuse that I took from my own father when I was pregnant with my daughter.

I was going to start a new life with a new person in a Mother and Infant Program, a place for young teenage mothers who have no home. But as I started my new life, I found myself putting off everything I had been saying about the way I would treat my child.

Anasia was 1½ months old when I hit her for the first time. I hit her because she kept crying for no reason and I thought hitting her would make her stop.

When Anasia turned 2 months old, the hitting increased and I also started screaming at her.

And when she was 3 months old, Anasia fell off her high-rise bed. She was crying and crying, and I left her on the floor to cry. I didn't pick her up until I was ready to get out of my own bed.

I kept asking myself, "Why do I keep hitting her?" I didn't know if I was hitting her because her father wasn't around or because I couldn't face being a teenage mother.

(Now, as I look back on the past, I think it also had to do with being put in foster care. I had never had to deal with any rules and regulations before, and it made me stress out.)

When Anasia was 9 or 10 months old, she had a seizure in my arms. I didn't know if it was because I was hitting her too much or because I wasn't feeding her enough. (To tell you the truth, I really didn't give a damn what it was from.) Half of me wanted to hurry up and take her to the hospital, and the other half was saying, "No, don't take her, let her die because you don't want her."

While I was taking my time to decide what to do, I was looking at this person in my arms. Her eye was closed up, her lips were blue from not getting enough air, and her body was shaking. I finally made up my mind to take her to the hospital and leave her there, so that's what I did.

The doctors rushed Anasia out of my arms and took her to another room. I stood in the emergency room for about five or 10 minutes, then I turned around and walked away. As I did I heard Anasia start to cry, but I tried to pay it no mind. Then she started to cry even louder and the people in the emergency room were looking at me in a funny way.

So I couldn't help but turn around and go into the hospital to see what was wrong with her. But I was just pretending, so I could make myself look like a good and concerned mother.

As I entered the room she was in, Anasia had lots of I-V tubes in her arms and legs and an oxygen mask over her face. Her eyes were so big. It seemed as if she was telling me to help her, with little tears in the corners of her eyes. I couldn't help but cry and ask myself, "Why?"

I told myself that I was never going to hit my child, because I didn't want her to experience the abuse that I took from my own father.

I knew that I needed help. I went and joined a group of teenagers called the Mentor's Group at an agency called Rosalie Hall, in the Bronx. They get together to discuss problems they're having and find ways to deal with them.

When I joined the Mentor's Group, I was afraid to tell them about the abuse I had done to my child. I don't know why, but as I started to listen to the stories that everyone was sharing with each other, I felt relieved and started opening up to them. Some of the things they were talking about I could relate to, such as being a single parent and raising a child in the system.

Then I caught myself and realized that nobody was sharing anything similar to what I had done to Anasia, so I felt that the group was not for me. But a young lady shared her experience of being abused mentally and physically (by either her mother or father, I can't remember) and after listening to her story, I couldn't help but to open up and tell them about what I had done to Anasia.

After I told my story, the group was quiet and didn't say anything at first. I thought they wouldn't understand me and were going to hate me, but I was wrong. They were quiet because of the abuse that I had done to my child, but also because they were trying to think of a way to help and support me in the best way they could.

The first thing they told me was that I had to stay with the hurt and not the anger. In other words, they were trying to say that if I was angry at my baby's father for leaving me, or if I was angry for being a mother at such a young age, I shouldn't take it out on Anasia. She didn't ask to be here, she didn't ask for anybody to hit or hate her, only to love her and show her the right way in life.

Listening to them made me feel so low about myself, because what they said was so powerful and so true. I had to accept the fact that Anasia was not the reason for my anger and should not be the target for it. That's a message that I've kept near to my heart, and it's made me become a better person. (Thanks guys.)

I try my best to put all the hitting and screaming behind us

Now that Anasia is 15 months she's getting into things, but I don't get the urge to hit or scream at her anymore. I try my best to put all the hitting and screaming behind us. I try to make up for the past by taking her to the park, playing pitty-patt with her, reading books to her at night, and showing her her eyes, nose, mouth, and ears, and telling her what they're used for.

If there was something that I could say to my daughter, it would be this: Anasia, there is a God, and He didn't let those foster people take you away from me. I believe in my heart that He's giving me a second chance to prove to you and to myself how much I love and appreciate you.

Love you, 'Nasia!

The author was 18 when she wrote this story.

Matty DeLuna

A Partner for Parents

By La'Quesha Barner

Not everybody plans on having a baby, and if you're not prepared, it's important to know that there are people out there who can help you. You don't have to be by yourself.

One place you can get help is the Nurse-Family Partnership, a national program that helps low-income, first-time mothers learn how to parent (www.nursefamilypartnership.org). You can sign up as soon as you know you're pregnant (but no later than the 28th week of your pregnancy). You'll be matched with a nurse who will visit you and your baby until the baby turns 2. I spoke with Julia Carter, a nurse who is now a supervisor in the New York City program, to find out more.

Q: How does the Nurse-Family Partnership work?

A: Each mom gets assigned a nurse, who is there to support the new mom. The nurse starts visiting with the mother while she's still pregnant and keeps working with her until the baby is 2 years old. Each visit lasts an hour and a half, and visits range from once a week to once a month, depending on how old the baby is.

Before the baby is born, the nurse helps the mom get prenatal care and tries to help her cut down on unhealthy habits like smoking.

Later, the nurse teaches her how to care for her baby. She helps the mother learn who her child is and how they can form a relationship.

Q: Who can join the program?

A: The Nurse-Family Partnership is open to any low-income pregnant woman who has never had a baby before. There are no age restrictions.

In October, we started a special project in New York City, which I'm supervising, to recruit girls who are in foster care, homeless or coming out of Rikers Island jail. We're targeting them because these moms are more vulnerable. They have all the questions any new mother would have, but less support.

Q: How are you recruiting teens in foster care?

A: That's the million dollar question! Teenagers in general are hard to reach, because they're often ambivalent about being pregnant—meaning they sometimes don't know if they want to keep the baby, and they tend not to tell adults that they're pregnant until the last minute.

In New York, we're trying to work with the youth development programs and at foster care agencies to reach teens in care. We try to go where teens are (whether they're pregnant or not) to let them know about the program, so that if they do become pregnant they might think of us.

Q: What happens if the mom doesn't have a stable home or is unhappy with her foster care placement—would you help her move to a better place?

A: We wouldn't do it for her, but we do try to work with the mother to help her find resources and navigate the system. A mom who's referred to us would already be connected to a social service agency like ACS, or the Department of Homeless Services, so she already has a social worker to advocate for her needs. The role of the nurse is to keep her connected to that person and those services.

Q: How much are fathers involved in the program?

A: The nurse visits the mom, but fathers are involved as much as the mother wants them to be. They too can learn parenting skills. In fact the nurse encourages fathers, family members and even friends to be involved. We'll work with whomever the mom identifies as her support.

Q: Can the mother call the nurse if there is an emergency? Would the nurse go to her house?

The nurse is there to support the new mom. She helps the mother learn who her child is and how they can form a relationship.

A: A mother can always call the nurse—they all have work cell phones—but that doesn't mean the nurse will always come to her client's house. The goal of the program really is to get the mom to be able to advocate for herself.

If a mom called in the middle of the night with a problem, the nurse would probably speak with her and help her figure out the best solution. It's empowering for the mom to be in the midst of an emergency and be able to find a solution.

Q: What happens if there are personal problems between the nurse and the mother?

A: Just like in any relationship, if there are problems we try to talk them out and come to some sort of solution. In a worst case scenario where the nurse and client just can't get along and it's not working, we may try to find a different nurse for the client, because we want her to have this program. But we try to handle personal differences without having to resort to that.

Q: What are the hardest things for new parents to learn?

A: I think the hardest thing for any new parent is realizing that this little baby is a person, with its own personality. As new parents, you have to learn to work with that personality so that you can communicate and understand what your baby needs from you. I think when things go wrong is when there's no communication.

Q: What happens to the parents after the two years of nurse care? Are they on their own then?

A: It's a relationship, so even once the program is over the nurse and the mom may stay in touch. But by the end of the program, the mom should be able to advocate for herself in a way she never would have been able to before. The nurse helps the mom to increase her self-esteem and identify her own support systems, so it's not such a big drop at the end of two years.

Q: Do any of the parents come back after their kids are adults to let you know how they're doing?

A: Nationally we follow the kids who are now adults, and our research has shown that these adults are more likely to be in college and to have jobs, and they have fewer incidents of juvenile delinquency and arrest—overall, they do better than the kids we've tracked whose mothers were not in the program.

Q: How could a pregnant teen sign up for this program?

A: In New York City, you can call 311 and someone will direct you to your closest site. Outside of New York, you can find out if a Nurse-Family Partnership program exists in your city by visiting our website, at www.nursefamilypartnership.org.

La'Quesha was 16 when she wrote this story.

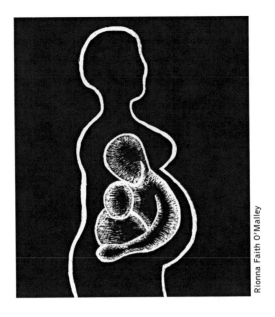

Rionna Faith O'Malley

My Teen Body
Wasn't Ready For Pregnancy

By Lillian Cremedy

People say that young teens are more at risk for having medical and physical complications during pregnancy than adults. I guess I'm proof of that because I'm a teen and having my daughter was real hectic.

When I was about 5½ months pregnant, I started to have contractions and go into false labor. From then on, my pregnancy was nothing but problems. I was put on so much medication and got stuck so many times with needles (which I'm afraid of) that I thought I would die. I went through so much pain and was rushed to the hospital so many times that it occurred to me that my body wasn't really ready to carry a child.

My school was upset that I kept going to the hospital because someone from the school had to come with me. So eventually they told me not to come back to school until after I had my baby. In a way, I was relieved when they said that. I would no longer have to get up every morning and try to get to school even when I didn't feel well.

Soon after my school told me to stay home, my doctor started putting me on bed rest for a couple of days at a time. I was so bored those days. There was nothing to do. But on the days that I went to the doctor, I couldn't return to my apartment until night. That was because my foster mother wouldn't give me keys. Once I left, I was locked out for the day. I would just go to my foster care agency and wait for night, when my foster mother got home. This went on until the end of my eighth month and it wasn't fun, to say the least.

From the end of my eighth month of pregnancy until I had my daughter, I was in the hospital about twice a week. One day the doctor told me that my child was underweight. I was devastated. I thought, "I gained all this weight for nothing?!" I started to stuff my face with food like crazy. I didn't have much of an appetite, but I wanted to get my baby's weight up.

I started having contractions about a week before my due date. Once more, I rushed to the hospital. The nurses said

My body wasn't really ready to carry a child.

that I had started to dilate. It was about time! But I hadn't dilated enough to deliver my daughter, so they sent me home to bed. Again.

Over the weekend I started feeling really sick. My water started leaking and I had a fever. Soon I had contractions again. I rushed to the hospital. The hospital staff wanted me to dilate even more before giving birth. They told me to wait in the hospital.

The pain started getting to me so much that I asked for drugs. When the doctor and nurses left to get me some anesthesia, I felt like I had to move my bowels, so I got up, held onto the back of the bed, and began to strain.

Just then the nurses and doctor came back in the room. They looked frantic and said, "No, no, don't do that! The baby is on the way. Lie back down." Then someone shouted, "I see the head!" I thought I was having a bowel movement, but really I had been birthing my daughter!

It was another 20 minutes or so before I pushed my daughter out completely. When she came out you could see this red line going around her head. It was from my pelvic bone, which her head had been resting on for about ten minutes.

The hospital staff wouldn't let me hold her because I was running a high fever and my daughter had already caught part of the infection that was causing my fever, so she went straight into an incubator. I couldn't hold her until my fever went down, which didn't go away for a few more days. When I finally did hold her, I was proud but relieved—finally, I was done being pregnant.

Read Lillian's story about finding a home for herself and her baby, starting on the next page.

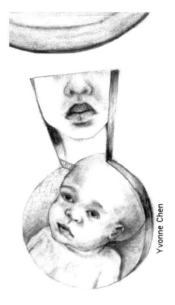

Yvonne Chen

It Took Five Tries To Find a Home

By Lillian Cremedy

I'm a teen mom in care, and it's been hard for me to find a good place for my daughter and me to live. I moved twice when I was pregnant, and twice since my baby was born. That's a lot of moving for a pregnant teen or a mom with her newborn.

I didn't move because I like moving. I moved because so many of my placements weren't good. I wanted to live in a home where my child and I could feel comfortable and be healthy. I wanted to feel at home in the placement, or at least come close to that feeling.

When I found out I was pregnant, I was living in an overcrowded house. It was a three-bedroom apartment packed with seven people and another on the way—my baby. I felt that there just wouldn't be enough room for a baby, too, so I knew I should move before I gave birth. That way I would have a home set up when she arrived.

Although it was overcrowded, I liked that home. I got along with everyone there and we were almost like family. I even told people that my foster mother was my aunt. But I thought I needed to have more space for my daughter and me.

So not long after I became pregnant, I found a new foster home. I found it myself—I had stayed there temporarily once before. The foster mother had seen that I was pregnant and said that she liked taking babies and little kids. So when I needed a new place to live, I asked her to take me and my soon-to-be-born daughter. She said that she was not used to taking teenagers but she'd take me because she knew me.

Now I wish she had just said no from the beginning, because after about a month we weren't getting along. She wouldn't give me keys to the house because she said that only adults get keys and I was just a child. I didn't have a problem with not having keys as long as she was home to let me in the apartment when I needed to get in. But a lot of the time she wasn't home and I would get locked out. Every time I got locked out, I would call or visit my agency so they would know what was happening in my foster home. Sometimes I spent whole afternoons at my agency, waiting for my foster mother to get home.

Other times, when my foster mother was home, she didn't answer the phone when I called. During that time, which was late in my pregnancy, I was having a lot of medical problems. I was in the hospital all the time. But when I called my foster mother and told her I was having a medical emergency, she still wouldn't pick up the phone. It seemed like she just didn't care and that upset me. So I decided to find a new home where people cared about me and my health.

It was hard trying to find a third home. I watched as my social worker called home after home, but most people didn't want a mother and child. Those who wanted us didn't have the space. Finally, after about a week, my social worker found a place for me. By this time I was very close to giving birth.

I gave birth to my daughter while living in that home. I hoped I had finally found a place to stay so I didn't have to keep adjusting to new places. But guess what? That home didn't work out, either.

I kept being locked out in the winter with my newborn. It was freezing cold, and my baby and I would get sick. It's one thing to lock out a teen, but to lock out a newborn baby is crazy and sickening.

What could I do? I had a baby now and didn't think it would be good for either of us to keep bouncing from one

I wanted to live in a home where my child and I could feel comfortable and be healthy.

home to another. So I thought long and hard about it and moved back to the home where I was living when I first became pregnant—the crowded one where I liked the people. By this time there were even more people living there than before, but I realized I would rather be in a place that's crowded instead of one where I'm not being treated well.

When my daughter was six months old, I was accepted into the Supervised Independent Living Program (SILP). Now I live in an apartment run by the agency. I like it there a lot. It's just me, my roommate, and our kids. Our social worker comes and checks up on us. I have been living here for about a year now. This is good because my daughter and I are more stable than before. My daughter knows where home is, where the train station is, who she lives with, and we both have enough space. Now that I don't have to worry so much about where we live, I can focus more on being a good mother.

The next time I move it will be out of foster care and into my own apartment. I don't want my daughter to have to keep moving like I did. I want her to be stable.

Lillian was a high school student when she wrote this story and the previous one.

James Faber

Where the Fathers At?

By Antwaun Garcia

My father is the type of male who is cool as a friend but sucky when it comes to taking care of his kids. Yeah, he was there sometimes, no complaints, but he was never there when I really needed him.

Living poor in the Harlem neighborhood of New York City, my father was always in and out of jail or handling business. I'm not blaming him for me ending up in foster care, but he could have made things easier for my family to stay together.

So many fathers like him lay down these kids and then leave them like nothing. So many males are ready and willing to have sex, but when something comes up and their mate says, "I'm pregnant, and it's yours," brothers be ready to flip. They either don't have much to do with the baby or claim it isn't theirs.

From what I've seen, the majority of the time the baby is theirs. So many mothers go with the grief of raising their child alone, and the child is left in confusion. That child might grow up hating his parents, because his single mother is going to do something stupid and there's no father to catch the kid's fall. Then the kid goes into foster care, like I did.

So now I'm asking, "Where the fathers at? Why aren't they doing more to help families stay together?"

Recently, I got a view of a teen father who's trying to raise his kids. I interviewed Ahlvoid, a black father from the streets of the Bronx who has two sons from two different mothers. Ahlvoid doesn't see enough of one of his sons because he doesn't live with the mother, which is a drag, but he's there day and night for his other son.

Ahlvoid talked about his own childhood growing up without a father, and how that made him determined to be the type of dad who is there for his kids.

As a child, Ahlvoid went through many struggles. When he was 3 his father passed away, leaving Ahlvoid with only the memories his family tells him about his father.

After his father's death, things went downhill. Ahlvoid grew up poor, as his mother struggled to make ends meet. Then she gave up and went on welfare. Eventually Ahlvoid and his baby sister moved in with their aunt.

At 10, Ahlvoid's mother got remarried to his stepfather, and they found a house to rent. Ahlvoid and his sister finally went back home and reunited with their mother. In his words, "I was happy as hell, very happy to be back with the family."

But things weren't going to be easy. Soon after they came home, Ahlvoid, who was now in junior high school, came to realize that his mother and her new husband were substance abusers. This made being at home less than pleasant, and soon things started getting out of hand. For one, there wasn't enough money for the family.

Eventually Ahlvoid got tired of the bull and turned his life to the streets in a desperate pursuit of money. He started to carry guns and began selling crack.

During this time his oldest sister, who was still a teen, became a crack addict. She would do the usual crackhead things, like steal from the family, sell their possessions, all that and more. So Ahlvoid's stepfather kicked her out of the house. "I didn't know the effects of drugs then," Ahlvoid remembers about that time. "I knew she wasn't acting right and I wanted to help, but I couldn't, so I felt helpless. I was feeling like I wasn't being a brother."

Ahlvoid decided that his girlfriend's pregnancy was a sign to finally get his life together.

Ahlvoid slowly started to realize how his new job—selling crack—was ruining the lives of many people, including those he loved. Around that time, his parents got evicted from their home and Ahlvoid found himself living in a shelter. The combination of all the bad things going down made him want to take a different path. He stopped selling and decided to go back to school, but then he dropped out again. Then, when he was 17, his girlfriend got pregnant.

It was a turning point in Ahlvoid's life—for the better. Instead of running away from the situation like so many other males do, Ahlvoid decided that his girlfriend's pregnancy was a sign to finally get his life together and get off the streets. He thought, "It's time to act my age and not my shoe size."

But he knew that at his age, he and his girlfriend needed help if they were going to raise a baby. Ahlvoid looked for and received love and support from his moms, sister, aunts, uncles, friends, grandparents, and more.

"I can always remember what my family told me, and it made me stronger," Ahlvoid remembers. "My mother told me, 'You can do it.' My sister said, 'Never do the things I do, I already done them for you.'"

Ahlvoid decided to set himself on the right path and joined the Youth Action Program, a counseling program where teen fathers can discuss their struggles.

Ahlvoid had a lot of struggles in his life even without the pregnancy—he had no GED, he was working at Burger King where he didn't make too much money, and his moms was still on welfare. So when Ahlvoid first went into the program, it was hard for him to think it was a good use of his time. "I felt out of place," he said. "I felt like dropping out. But I had to strive on."

Eventually Ahlvoid began to see that the program could help him a lot. He received support from the group leaders, who helped him sign up for programs to learn computer skills and leadership abilities. Ahlvoid's life felt on the right track by the time his girfriend had her baby.

Ahlvoid was there to see the birth of his baby boy. "It was a nasty, but a beautiful sight," he said. Ahlvoid knew he was better prepared to be a father than he had been several months ago, but he was still a little uncertain. Soon, though, he realized he loved being a father. He loved watching his baby grow and discover the world.

But it wasn't long before Ahlvoid's relationship with his girl went kind of rocky. He remembers, "I wanted to be a playa, live the fast life. But I just ended up being hurt."

He and his girlfriend separated, though Ahlvoid tried to continue being there for his son. He found himself a new girl, and shortly afterwards she announced her pregnancy. Luckily, this girl was financially stable and didn't need much help from Ahlvoid in that area. But he was worried about how he was going to be there for two children who live in two different homes.

Soon his second son was born. Times were tough for Ahlvoid, as he tried to juggle being a father to two sons with two different mothers. He couldn't believe how many diapers both his sons used, and how much they cost. And he knew he couldn't keep running between the two mothers. He had to choose one to be with. He said, "I made my decision by what I felt in my heart."

Ahlvoid kept his love for his first girl, and moved into a house with her and their 2-year-old son. Their relationship wasn't always easy, and at times he regretted that he couldn't live with both his sons in one place.

But his schedule with one son was tough. He or his girl would have to get up in the middle of the night whenever the baby cried. "Then, when you finally think you're getting some sleep," he said, "about 3:30 in the morning my girl would throw her elbows at my side, telling me to get the baby because he's crying again."

He couldn't believe how many diapers both his sons used, and how much they cost.

After a night of little sleep, Ahlvoid would wake up at 5:30 in the morning to start his day. Around 6 a.m. "your alarm clock [the baby] would sound off. Then I'd hurry to get his milk and start to get him dressed, while my girl is in the shower getting herself ready for the day."

After a full day of work he spends some of his early evenings with the Youth Action Program. But usually he comes home around 5:30 p.m., to ask his fiancé about her day and spend time with his son.

To help him through the tough times, Ahlvoid has started turning to God for advice and support. He wants assurance from God that he will be able to be there for his two sons "fully to death."

Ahlvoid wishes he had more time to himself, and is trying to get an education so that his sons can have a better future. He sees himself becoming either a social worker or a plumber. "Hopefully, at a certain age, I can be an old fart," he said, "just making money, sitting at home watching TV."

Males like Ahlvoid who stand by their kids and provide for their family are setting a good example for the hard-headed males out there who don't do for their seed. Those males who do take care of their responsibility in a respectful manner are, in my opinion, helping to reduce the number of children being placed in foster care.

Antwaun was 17 when he wrote this story.
He later attended LaGuardia Community College.

Asaiah Aajibabi

Growing Up Together

By Vanessa Sanchez

One day I went to the supermarket with my 3-year-old son, John, and he started screaming at the top of his lungs. I tried to remain calm.

"John, do you really think that's necessary?" I asked. "Do you even know why you're crying?" But that didn't stop him. He cried as if someone was beating him.

It felt like we had a huge, bright spotlight on us in the middle of the jam-packed supermarket. My friend, who was shopping with me, slowly but surely drifted away, as if she was not with us. Everything seemed like a blur of embarrassment as my son cried and cried.

I didn't know what to do. I moved into an empty aisle and started yelling with a stern voice. "If you do not be quiet, I will leave you right here on your own!"

Finally, I took a deep breath, hugged my son, and said, "I love you, John. You are embarrassing the both of us, so if there is something you need, you have to say it, because I cannot understand you when you're crying."

"I'm tired, mommy," John replied.

"It can't be it was that simple, John," I sighed, but it was. So I removed my coat and made it into a pillow for him in the shopping cart.

Sometimes it is extremely difficult to handle my son's temper along with mine. The good things—that smile he has, the moments when we connect—keep me going.

I was 18 when I found out I was pregnant with my son. I was one of those stupid little teenagers who wanted a baby because I thought it would be cute. I didn't know then how difficult it would be to raise a child on my own, how there would be times where I would feel lonelier than I ever had before in my life, with no one to blame but myself because I made the decision to have a baby.

When I got pregnant, I was determined to prove to myself that I could be a better mother to John than my own mother had been to me. My mom used drugs when I was a child, and my childhood was sad and embarrassing, from the beatings she gave me to the jokes at

Sometimes I catch myself doing the same things I hated in my mother.

school for wearing Payless shoes. My mother was so caught up in her drug habit that our Christmas gifts were given to us and sold in the same day.

I want to prove to myself and other people that growing up in a negative environment doesn't mean you can't flourish. I will raise my son without abusing him in any way, and finish college and pursue a career as a nurse.

To prepare to be a mother, I participated in parenting classes and read books about parenting. I remember sitting on the bus and seeing this woman giving her son a slap on the hand because he was jumping on the seats. "That's not how I am going to be with my child," I said to myself. "He's going to listen, and we're only going to have to sit and talk about discipline for him to follow what I say."

Yeah, right. Little did I know it wasn't that easy.

The first few months after John was born were a lot harder than I expected. You know, with a newborn, you're lucky if you get a full three hours of sleep. One day John just started crying and crying. I had no idea what was wrong. I mean, I burped, changed, fed, and rocked him, but nothing helped.

Finally, I had no choice but to put him down and walk away because I was literally shaking and dizzy. It took a while before I pulled myself together and said, "If I don't do it, no one else will." I got up, grabbed my baby, and paced for about an hour more before he stopped crying.

About two months after John was born, I was finally catching some ZZZs, but I was already behind in college by the time John was 2. Taking care of my baby, working, and going to school turned out to be nearly impossible, and I put school off.

I know I have to keep growing, to be the mother I want to be.

Now John is 3 years old. He has a big head topped off with a mat of brown hair, big brown eyes, and two handfuls of cheeks. His little voice brings me an array of feelings, from joy to frustration. I find my son more interesting now because he is learning and has more to say. He is also tougher to discipline. I say, "John, don't do that." He says, "You don't do that!"

I love my son but, boy, does he do some things. I get repeated complaints from the teacher: "Your son is being disruptive" or "John does not focus on his work."

One day John's teacher said he hit a little girl and she put him on time out. John was so angry that he kept cutting the teacher off to say, "But mom, Victoria bump me with her butt against the wall!" I wasn't sure who to believe, but I was upset that my baby kept getting into trouble.

I requested an evaluation through the Board of Education, only to find that nothing was wrong with him. I worry, though, because my son's father was very disruptive in school. I am so afraid of my son possibly repeating negative patterns of behavior on my side of the family or on his father's. Any bad behavior causes me to think he's going to end up in serious trouble.

Maybe I should consider that my son is just a 3-year-old boy who likes to play more than he likes to sit and write the letters of the alphabet. The evaluator even suggested that he might do better in a pre-school that's more about playing and less like school.

Sometimes I catch myself doing the same things I hated in my mother. Because of her addiction, my mom was inconsistent. I felt frustrated that I couldn't count on her to cook when I was hungry or help me do my homework. She disciplined my siblings and me when it wasn't necessary, and let us get away with things when we needed discipline.

Inconsistency is mistake number one that I make with my son today. If John jumps on the bed I punish him, but if I'm on the phone and he jumps on the bed then I completely disregard it. I know consistency is difficult, especially for a single parent, but I feel upset that I'm not on top of things as much as I'd like to be.

Sometimes I just feel overwhelmed. One day I was arguing with John's father while cooking some sausages on the stove. When they started to burn I said, "I'm not dealing with that," but he did nothing. Smoke started to fill the kitchen. I got so mad that I flung the pot against the kitchen door.

My son was watching cartoons in the next room and walked out to see sausages on the floor and his mommy upset.

"What happened, ma? You all right?" he asked. I quickly had to grab my composure and say yes. I thought, "He's going to learn that this is how to react to anger." That really bothered me. I felt embarrassed that I'd lost control.

What I've learned is that parenting is all about confusion. I'm always confused about little things, like whether I should give John a time out, or whether to give him juice when bedtime is around the corner. Should I say no, or do I say no too often?

I'm also confused about the big things: which school to put him in, whether John is learning the right behavior from me, and whether he's growing into a good kid.

I look for signs that John is doing well. I see that John has good qualities: he's loving and helpful and very entertaining. Our communication has developed so we understand each other better now.

Just the other day I was sick and he came and rubbed my back, saying, "Mommy, you all right?" I was feeling half-dead, but I was able to crack a smile, because my baby came along with a thermometer saying, "Turn over, mommy, I'll help you."

Now I understand why people say, "You're too young!" Being a single mother is something you need to be mentally prepared for. My advice to other girls is to wait.

But I also like that my son is here with me through my own years of growing. I started college again in the fall, and over my winter break I kept John home from pre-school most days. I wanted the extra time with him. I am bored at home with no one to tell "Stop that!" or "Come play ball with me."

There are times when John and I are home and I say to myself, "Wow, my baby is growing so fast." I know I have to keep growing at a fast pace, too, to be the mother I want to be. I'm determined to set us both on the right path and make my son proud. John will be there to see me finish college and will be learning from me as I start a career.

Vanessa wrote this article for Rise, *a magazine written by parents involved in the foster care system.*

Nelle McKay

A Mother's Touch

By Natasha Santos

One afternoon last spring, eight teens gathered in a circle for a class on baby massage at Inwood House, a group home for pregnant and parenting teens in New York City. Amy Cooper, a therapist, had come from California to teach massage to moms in foster care.

Amy had a calm voice and mild manner. She told the group that baby massage is a way to help moms and their babies more strongly connect. It's a good tool to help regulate your baby's tension and stress, and helps babies sleep more and cry less.

One girl in the group seemed really surprised and slightly nervous about the idea that babies liked to be touched.

"Some of us have negative experiences with touch, like if it was used to punish us," Amy said. She suggested that baby massage could be therapeutic: "To moms who haven't had good experiences, baby massage can be a positive way to respond to your baby when he or she is upset. Rather than neglecting or hurting your baby, you could massage. It's like changing the cycle."

All of the girls in the group were pregnant, except the mother of 7-month-old Madison. When her mom tried to begin giving her a massage, Madison wasn't too attentive. She was more interested in the taste and feel of her feet, and kept putting them in her mouth. Finally, Madison's mom placed her hands on Madison's belly. Madison made eye contact with her mom when she did that and her mom was able to begin the massage.

Amy used a baby doll to demonstrate some massage techniques for the stomach, arms, legs, and chest. She said that it was good to get a non-petroleum-based oil (like vegetable or olive oil) so your touch feels smooth to the baby.

Start by rubbing your hands together and asking your baby permission to perform the massage, even if the baby can't respond yet. "You want to make sure that your baby is ready to receive touch," she said.

Some techniques she showed us were simple, like Indian Milking, which is using two hands to firmly but gently rub your baby's leg from the hip to the ankle. Walking was also very simple—with your palms on the top of your baby's foot, use your two thumbs to walk from the heel of his/her foot to the toes. Amy said there are thousands of nerves in the feet so it can be very relaxing. A good way to relax the joints (ankles, wrists, and knees) is by firmly but gently making small circles around them with your thumb and index finger.

The face massages are pretty easy, like the Open Book, which is rubbing your fingers back and forth from your baby's brow to the temple. You can gently rub your thumb over your baby's eyes if he or she permits it. For sinuses, you can gently push up on the bridge of the nose and then down across the cheek. When massaging your baby's face, don't use any oil and avoid feathering the cheeks (light brushing with fingertips). That tickles and isn't relaxing.

Amy also showed us some back massages. Rubbing both of your hands back and forth across the back is relaxing for babies. Swooping your hands to their bottoms or ankles is also very good.

Amy told us that babies communicate with you and their environment through body language. She explained that when a baby is communicating irritation or annoyance, it's usually because the baby is over-whelmed or uncomfortable, not because they don't like you.

Massage helps babies sleep more and cry less.

"Some of us get disappointed when we're looking at our baby and he or she looks away. It's not that they're rejecting you, but they're saying 'That was a lot to take in, give me a moment.'" Amy said that, like us, babies have their boundaries of closeness and comfort.

She demonstrated this with one of the girls. She asked the girl to walk toward her, and when Amy felt uncomfortable with the closeness, she told her to stop. Then she and the girl switched roles. The girl definitely preferred more space than Amy! We all giggled, but it was true—people have their own boundaries that make them feel comfortable.

Amy emphasized that massage is a way for both the baby and the mom to relax. She told the girls that it's important that they take care of themselves, too. Amy suggested that singing is a good way to relax yourself and your baby before and during a massage. At the end of our class, she asked us to put one hand on our bellies and the other on our hearts while singing "Twinkle, Twinkle Little Star."

"No matter how well or how badly you sing, your baby loves your voice," she said, explaining that studies show that babies recognize their mothers' voices.

Toward the end of her massage, Madison got restless and

began giggling. She squirmed while her mom tried to massage her face, and her mom had to stop.

"That's OK," Amy said. She explained that massage is simply a way of connecting and relaxing, and every baby has her own limits. "She's showing you she's had enough."

For more information on massage techniques, you can visit www.makewayforbaby.com. You might also want to check out the book *Baby Massage: The Calming Power of Touch*, by Alan Heath and Nicki Bainbridge.

Natasha was 19 when she wrote this story.
She later attended the University of New Orleans.

Family Man

By Mimi Callaghan with Lenny Jones

Max Soto used to live a wild life. He would hang in the streets with older crowds and drink beer. Sometimes he would even rob people.

"My friend and I had this gig," said Max. "If we put fear in people's hearts, we would get paid. They used to be scared to see me and my friend coming down the block. They already had their money in their hands. And I don't care if it was a dollar or 50 cents, give me something."

All that changed when Max became a father while he was still in high school.

Although his first impulse was to run from the responsibility, Max eventually joined the young fathers program at Inwood House, a group home for pregnant and parenting teens in New York City, and found the support he needed to turn his life around. With help, he became the father he always wished he'd had growing up.

By the time he joined the program, Max had two children by two different girls, and his current girlfriend was pregnant for the second time.

Max's kids were on welfare and Max was on probation, and he wasn't sure he would finish high school. He didn't know what to do with his life.

"I had all these things coming at me at once, so, you know, it was hard for me," Max said. "It was a lot of stress for me, you know what I'm saying? I was overwhelmed."

But Max's life now is very positive—and extremely busy. He is in his third year of college and works part time at a crisis intervention center.

He has no time to hang out or do the wrong thing. He doesn't even have time to be with friends. And he doesn't mind it.

"I'm a family man, and that's it," said Max. "The best part about being a father is the kids, man. Before I leave, they always want to give me a kiss, all the time. They never let me walk out the house without giving me a kiss."

Max is determined to be a real father to his children—a father who spends his time with his kids and is involved in their lives.

"I don't want them to grow up the way I did, without no money, without no support," Max said.

Still, Max regrets that he isn't too close with his first child, Ricky, who is now 7. When Ricky's mom told Max she was pregnant, Max was only 16. His first reaction was shock and denial.

"I was like, what? I ain't ready for this," Max said. "I was telling her to take it out, to tell the truth. I was like, 'Yo, you can't have this kid.'"

Max felt like she was trying to trap him. He felt like the world was going to end.

"My mentality wasn't like it is now. My mentality before was, I just wanted a hit. I just wanted her for her skin," Max said. "I never loved her. I never even made her my girl. Until all of a sudden she was pregnant—and she became my girlfriend and all this stuff started coming."

Max was desperate not to be a father. He would tell his girlfriend that he had other girlfriends to upset her. He knew it was wrong, but he didn't care.

Then she almost lost the baby and Max had a change of heart. He started to have feelings for the baby.

"My life changed, you know, when I had my first kid," Max said. "I was like, 'Wow, I've got a kid to take care of.' "

At the same time, Max was thinking about how his youth would be gone. He knew he would have a lot of responsibilities, and he didn't even know how he was going to pay for Pampers or to feed Ricky.

At times he didn't have enough money to buy his child milk. Instead, he had to steal it.

After his first son was born, Max got a job at a library. It didn't pay much at all, only $150 every two weeks. However, it gave him some money to support his child. Max said the mother of his first child didn't appreciate what he was trying to do.

Once he brought home two packages of Pampers for his son, and she said, "Oh, that's all you could afford?" It made Max feel bad that he couldn't do more.

Max became the father he always wished he'd had growing up.

Now when he talks about his ex-girlfriend, he says, "We don't get along, period." He says not being with her makes it harder to have a close relationship with his son.

After Max had Ricky, he began to take life more seriously. He found a girlfriend he was committed to, and he learned how to hold down a job. Still, it took him a long time to get himself on track. Max knew he didn't want to have another child, but he still didn't use protection.

When Max was 18, his new girlfriend, Cathy, got pregnant. He didn't want her to have the child. They decided that she would have an abortion and even went to a clinic to have it done. But at the last minute Cathy changed her mind and ran out of the place.

They had the baby, Stephanie, and two years later Cathy got pregnant again. While Cathy was pregnant with Alize, their second child together, she joined a program for teen mothers at Inwood House.

At that time, Inwood House was just starting a young fathers program. Max was under a lot of stress and needed someone to talk to. That someone was Ben Powell, who ran the fathers program.

Ben was there for Max. He was an ear, a father figure, a friend, an uncle—whatever Max needed him to be.

At Inwood House, Max also met other young fathers. They were going through the same things he was and some of them had it even worse. Knowing that others were struggling like he was kept Max from feeling like a failure when things weren't going well for him.

Max knew he didn't want to have another child, but he still didn't use protection.

Once, soon after he graduated from high school, Max went for a job interview and got in an argument with the interviewer. Of course, he didn't get the job.

Upset and scared, Max called Ben for help.

"I was like, 'Oh, dip, I just came out of high school, I don't have no job.' I was so frustrated 'cause I wasn't going to have no income," said Max. "I just said, 'Damn, nothing works out for me, man, I'm gonna give up.' "

Ben encouraged Max to keep looking for a job, and eventually, he even convinced him to go to college—something which Max had never imagined he could do.

Ben helped Max by listening and by making Max help himself. When Max started thinking about college, he wanted Ben to go with him to get information. But Ben wanted Max to be independent and know that he could accomplish whatever he wanted, so he made him go by himself. Eventually, Max applied and was accepted to Monroe College.

While he was in college, Max got a job as a maintenance worker at a crisis intervention center. He was making very little money, and he sometimes thought about quitting.

But when a job as a counselor opened up during his second year of school, he applied and was hired.

"I went from cleaning to helping people, which is what I really want to do," Max said.

When he was in high school, Max didn't have any faith in himself or any dreams for his future. He never imagined that he could go to college and support a family. He didn't think he could do much of anything.

"When I was growing up, I didn't see beyond the Bronx and Manhattan," Max said. "I felt like, 'This is it, I'm stuck right here. I'm stuck in the ghetto part of life.' "

At Inwood House, Max built up his self-esteem, and now he feels like there is nothing that can stop him from doing whatever he wants.

"I needed somebody like Ben to give me the words of encouragement and make me believe in myself," he said.

Now Max lives with Cathy and their two kids, Stephanie, 4, and Alize, 2. He also pays child support for Ricky.

Max feels especially devoted to his children because he grew up without his real father, and he always wished his father had stuck around. His family was never really there to guide him. He had to learn stuff on his own.

The hopes Max has for his children inspired him to go to college, so he will be able to make his children's lives easier. And it's not simply the financial support that makes Max a good father—he spends time with his kids and shows them he loves them.

"People think just because they pay child support, they're being a father," Max said. "But being a father is being with your kids, taking them out, and giving them love."

Still, it's been really hard for Max to get to where he is. And while he doesn't regret his kids, he also suggests that teenagers use protection and wait until they're older to have a child.

"I love my kids to death," Max said. "But if I had the mentality I have now, I would wait. I'd first get my education. Once I had an education and a career going for myself, I would think about kids."

Mimi was 17 when she wrote this story. She later attended John Jay College. Lenny was 19 when he assisted with this story. As a researcher for travel books, he has traveled extensively around the world.

Marc Mazurkiewicz

Will I Get My Children Back?

By Jessica DeSince

When I was 16, I became pregnant. After my son Edwin was born and was about 11 months old, I started hanging out all night long. I was coming home at all hours.

I was living with my grandmother at the time and decided that I didn't want to live by her rules, so I moved into a friend's house. That's why my grandmother put out a PINS warrant (Person in Need of Supervision) on me.

I went into foster care that same night. Now I had to live by someone else's rules—or else. I had to stop hanging out and do the right things in order to raise my son Edwin properly.

Well, I didn't do the right things. I continued to hang out after I went into foster care because I no longer wanted to live with my foster family. The end result was that I got pregnant and had a second child—a daughter named Shaquira—and both children were eventually taken away from me and put in a separate foster home. It was emotionally devastating to have my son and daughter taken away from me.

First, my son was separated from me because my agency said I was being "unknowingly neglectful." That means that, because of my age, I didn't know any better. They said I got my son sick because I kept going out at all hours of the night and taking him with me.

After Edwin was separated from me, I started seeing him once a week, at the agency on Tuesdays. At this point I was pregnant with my second child. I got pregnant while I was on the pill. I wasn't taking them properly. I forgot to take them sometimes, and then I had to take a backup pill the next day. I guess I did it too many times.

It hurt me to know I couldn't feed Edwin, couldn't braid his hair, couldn't tuck him in bed. I got to see him for only an hour each week. I cried and cried every time I went to see him. My social worker, Ms. F, told me that if I couldn't hold myself together in the presence of my son, she would stop my visits.

While I was pregnant, I was put in a group home/maternity shelter for women. I continued to go AWOL and not go to school. When I did go to school, I was asleep in class. Every day I went out to my boyfriend's house. And almost every day I came to the house after curfew. I did it because I wanted to be grown and I didn't want to listen to anyone but myself.

For six months I stayed at the maternity home. At the end of June, I was in my room and I felt my stomach get real hard (the same way it does when you start to have contractions). I went to the bathroom and I saw that I was bleeding a little bit.

I was more than seven and half months pregnant and I wasn't supposed to be bleeding at this stage of my pregnancy. I went downstairs to the staff and told them. It was about 11 or 12 o'clock. We went to the hospital.

They put me on monitors and they told me that I was having

contractions. The nurse told me that it was probably due to dehydration, and that I was going to be put on an I.V. I told her that I drank enough water. She replied that the I.V. normally stops the contractions.

When I left the hospital, the doctor put me on bed/pelvic rest. That meant I was to stay in bed, rest, and not have sex. I'm not proud to say that I didn't stay in bed. I went out against the rules. I hope you're not thinking I didn't care about my baby, because I did. A lot.

I couldn't feed Edwin, couldn't braid his hair, couldn't tuck him in bed.

You've got to look at it from my point of view—I was pregnant, miserable, and lonely. Being holed up in a house with other pregnant, miserable, and lonely teenagers wasn't my cup of tea. I needed to be with my man.

I ended up going into labor again less than two weeks later. They told me I was now on strict bed rest, which meant I wasn't to get up except to get food and use the bathroom.

I was still allowed to have weekly visits with my son, as long as I went in a cab. It was nearing Edwin's second birthday and I wanted to go see him. But my new social worker told me I couldn't see him because two days before I had gone AWOL. I started crying and carrying on.

The social worker finally told me that this was my last chance to get a day pass to see Edwin, and if I messed up I wouldn't get any more. I smiled, hugged her, and told her I wouldn't mess up.

But after seeing my son, I went to see my boyfriend. I don't know what made me do it. I just didn't want to go back to the house. I wanted to be with my boyfriend. I couldn't bear having to go back to a house full of pregos who were constantly bickering and at each other's throats.

My boyfriend asked me what was I doing at his house. The nurse had told me in front of him that I was to be on bed rest, as well as pelvic rest. We argued about it. He told me to go back to the maternity home, but in the end he let me have my way.

I ended up spending the weekend with my boyfriend. I didn't have my medicine and I persuaded my boyfriend into having sex with me. I went to lay down and watch TV. About five minutes later I heard a whooshing sound and my water broke.

I woke my boyfriend up and he called the ambulance. I ended up having my daughter Shaquira two days after Edwin's 2nd birthday, and two months ahead of time.

My daughter weighed three pounds eight ounces at birth. She was in the hospital for a month. She finally reached five pounds and was drinking from a bottle. She was discharged from the hospital into foster care's hands, and was placed with her brother in his foster home.

People make mistakes, sometimes more than once, but you've got to learn from them the first time.

I now get to see them both at the same time. It's hard for me to see them, knowing that because of my behavior, the three of us aren't together. I cry a lot about it, but crying doesn't make me feel better. It just seems that's all I can do.

The State charged me with neglect. I am presently in court trying to get my kids back. The State wants me to go to school, to come in by my curfew, obey my foster parents, attend parenting classes, and go to therapy in order to get my two children back. I think it's fair, since that's what I'm supposed to be doing anyway. I'm going to school and so far I'm doing the right things.

I'm trying to stress that people make mistakes, sometimes more than once, but you've got to learn from them the first time. You can't let them repeat over and over. You've got to learn the first time. It shouldn't have to get to a second time, because by then you could lose something that's very important to you, like I did.

I'm sharing my story to help anyone who is in my position, or who might end up in my position, because I want to warn people that these things can happen if you let them. If you do get pregnant again, don't have the child because "it just happened." Do it because you really want to have another child and are ready to take on the responsibility.

I thought the worst thing that ever happened to me was having to live in a stranger's house and abide by her rules. I was wrong, dead wrong. The worst thing ever to happen to me was having the child I lived with, slept with, and ate with taken away from me. Then to have a second child, who did not even know my scent yet, who had not yet spent a whole day with me, also taken from me.

I finished my parenting class last year and got a certificate for it. School has been just fine. I'm not an Einstein, but I'm passing. I've been coming in at decent hours and basically doing the right things. I hope to have both of my children back soon.

Jessica was 17 when she wrote this story.

Rafael Manashirov

How I Became
a Stronger Mother

By Anzula Richardson

There I was, back in foster care, but this time it was different—
I was pregnant. Rosalie Hall, in the Bronx, New York, was a
strange place. They told my mother it was a maternity residence,
but to me that was just a fancy name for a group home for pregnant girls.

I was two months pregnant and I would have to spend my
entire pregnancy there. I wanted to be back in Georgia with my
boyfriend Lorenzo. We were supposed to go through the pregnancy together. What would become of our relationship? Would
we be a real family?

All kinds of questions were running freely in my mind. So
many different feelings were jumbled up inside. I couldn't gather
them all together, or even begin to sort them out. I knew that the

social worker couldn't do that for me, either.

But thanks to the Mentor's Program at Rosalie Hall, I was able to begin to gather and sort out all my questions and feelings. They pulled me under their wing in the third month of my pregnancy. They began to help me face the decision I had made to keep my baby.

I can still remember Mr. Parker, the assistant director of Rosalie Hall, telling me that I was referred to the program because he thought I could benefit from it. I usually ask a lot of questions when I hear about something new, but for some reason I didn't care to know too much about the program.

Mr. Parker explained that the Mentor's Program was organized about three years ago to prevent teen pregnancy by having pregnant and parenting teens go out into the community and share their experiences with others, by speaking in front of groups of young people.

"And this is what you want me to do?" I said. "Well sure...I guess so." I can remember not really caring.

Peggy and Catrina, both teen mothers, were going to train and counsel me. They were supposed to help me write out what I wanted to share with the kids at a local girls' club. I was really nervous, not so much about speaking in front of people as about sharing my story.

I realized I was scared to death of becoming a mother.

That's when I realized I was scared to death of becoming a mother. But I also was sure my boyfriend was going to be there for the baby and me. I wasn't worried about finishing school, because my boyfriend had graduated and he had a good job. Why did I have to get a job?

Boy, did I have a lot to learn.

After hearing stories from other girls in the Mentor's Program, I had to check myself. One of the girls went through her entire pregnancy with her baby's father, but after the baby was born he no longer wanted the responsibility. Another girl was abandoned by her baby's father as soon as she told him she was pregnant. After hearing these stories, I had to reevaluate my relationship with Lorenzo.

Was I living in some fantasy world? Was having this baby the wrong decision? Some of the things one girl said about her baby's father sounded just like Lorenzo. Her baby's father was supportive of anything she did and was always right by her side. He did whatever he could for her, just like Lorenzo.

With their love and support, I've learned to be a stronger black mother and a much better person.

But would my boyfriend really be there for me?

Damn, I went into the program with a lot of questions and now I had even more.

My fifth month of pregnancy came around and I was snapped back into reality. Lorenzo had started to change. He didn't call or write as much as he did when I first left. When I would call him in Georgia he wasn't home, and his mother told me he was hanging out. This was taking a great toll on me.

But because some of the girls in the Mentor's Program had warned me, I was prepared to deal with it. They taught me that it was all right to be hurt, so I cried and felt better. They showed me through their own experiences and through my previous relationships that I could make it with or without Lorenzo.

Mr. Parker and some of the girls sat me down and asked me to make a list of my goals. I still have that list:

1. Have a healthy baby.
2. Go back home to Lorenzo.
3. Get a job.

Nowhere in my goals did I mention school or a career. They didn't point it out to me right then. But up until this very day they have been helping me set better goals for myself and my child. With their love and support, I've learned to be a stronger black mother and a much better person. My goals are much higher now:

1. Try my best to raise my son right, give him the right values and morals in life.

2. Graduate high school, and go on to a four-year college.

3. Get my master's in child psychology, and start my career as a child psychologist.

4. Buy my son and myself our first home.

5. And then maybe, just maybe, find a good husband who must also be a good stepfather.

I can remember the discussions we would have when we went to talk in the community. We would share stories about what happened when we found out we were pregnant. After we were finished, the audience would ask questions. For younger kids we would play a game called Sexual Jeopardy, which was like Jeopardy, but the questions were about sexual facts and myths. Or we did a skit. For the older kids we would usually have group discussions.

There was a time when I left the program. I had a bad experience with one of the groups I was talking to. They asked questions that were very personal, and they even got nasty when asking them.

I remember one young person asking me, "How do you feel now that you have to grow up along with your baby?" The kids made me feel stupid and depressed. They had me thinking about living in a shelter and they made me wonder why I was having my son.

The other mothers in the group understood. They told me to take the time I needed to decide if I could continue sharing my experiences as a pregnant teen. After I had my son, I returned to the program.

I decided to return because I had a long talk with Mr. Parker. He helped me realize that I could really help support another pregnant girl who is going through the things I went through and am still going through. The most important thing of all was that I realized that I needed the support of the program for myself.

I am still with the Mentor's Program and my dependency on Lorenzo has changed. You see, Lorenzo and I broke up a month after my son was born. It hurt and it still hurts (six months later), but at least now I am more self-sufficient than I was before. I am going to school, working with the Mentor's Program, and with my mother's help I am raising my son to the best of my ability.

I know now that when I'm confused and hurt I can get help from someone who cares, instead of not facing it. I think we all need support from somewhere. It doesn't matter whether it's a friend, a counselor, or a support group like mine, as long as someone is there to pick us up if we fall.

Anzula was 18 when she wrote this story.
She later joined the Navy.

Townsend Press

Lost and Found

Darcy Wills winced at the loud rap music coming from her sister's room.

My rhymes were rockin'
MC's were droppin'
People shoutin' and hip-hoppin'
Step to me and you'll be inferior
'Cause I'm your lyrical superior.

Darcy went to Grandma's room. The darkened room smelled of lilac perfume, Grandma's favorite, but since her stroke Grandma did not notice it, or much of anything.

"Bye, Grandma," Darcy whispered from the doorway. "I'm going to school now."

Just then, the music from Jamee's room cut off, and Jamee rushed into the hallway.

The teen characters in the Bluford novels, a fiction series by Townsend Press, struggle with many of the same difficult issues as the writers in this book. Here's the first chapter from *Lost and Found*, by Anne Schraff, the first book in the series. In this novel, high school sophomore Darcy contends with the return of her long-absent father, the troubling behavior of her younger sister Jamee, and the beginning of her first relationship.

"Like she even hears you," Jamee said as she passed Darcy. Just two years younger than Darcy, Jamee was in eighth grade, though she looked older.

"It's still nice to talk to her. Sometimes she understands. You want to pretend she's not here or something?"

"She's not," Jamee said, grabbing her backpack.

"Did you study for your math test?" Darcy asked. Mom was an emergency room nurse who worked rotating shifts. Most of the time, Mom was too tired to pay much attention to the girls' schoolwork. So Darcy tried to keep track of Jamee.

"Mind your own business," Jamee snapped.

"You got two D's on your last report card," Darcy scolded. "You wanna flunk?" Darcy did not want to sound like a nagging parent, but Jamee wasn't doing her best. Maybe she couldn't make A's like Darcy, but she could do better.

Jamee stomped out of the apartment, slamming the door behind her. "Mom's trying to get some rest!" Darcy yelled. "Do you have to be so selfish?" But Jamee was already gone, and the apartment was suddenly quiet.

Darcy loved her sister. Once, they had been good friends. But now all Jamee cared about was her new group of rowdy friends. They leaned on cars outside of school and turned up rap music on their boom boxes until the street seemed to tremble like an earthquake. Jamee had even stopped hanging out with her old friend Alisha Wrobel, something she used to do every weekend.

Darcy went back into the living room, where her mother sat in the recliner sipping coffee. "I'll be home at 2:30, Mom," Darcy said. Mom smiled faintly. She was tired, always tired. And lately she was worried too. The hospital where she worked was cutting staff. It seemed each day fewer people were expected to do more work. It was like trying to climb a mountain that keeps getting taller as you go. Mom was forty-four, but just yesterday she said, "I'm like an old car that's run out of warranty, baby. You know what happens then. Old car is ready for the junk heap. Well, maybe that hospital is gonna tell me one of these days—'Mattie Mae Wills, we don't need you anymore. We can get somebody younger and cheaper.'"

"Mom, you're not old at all," Darcy had said, but they were only words, empty words. They could not erase the dark, weary lines from beneath her mother's eyes.

Darcy headed down the street toward Bluford High School. It was not a terrible neighborhood they lived in; it just was not good. Many front yards were not cared for. Debris—fast food wrappers, plastic bags, old newspapers—blew around and piled against fences and curbs. Darcy hated that. Sometimes she and other kids from school spent Saturday mornings cleaning up, but it seemed a losing battle. Now, as she walked, she tried to focus on small spots of beauty along the way. Mrs. Walker's pink and white roses bobbed proudly in the morning breeze. The Hustons' rock garden was carefully designed around a wooden windmill.

As she neared Bluford, Darcy thought about the science project that her biology teacher, Ms. Reed, was assigning. Darcy was doing hers on tidal pools. She was looking forward to visiting a real tidal pool, taking pictures, and doing research. Today, Ms. Reed would be dividing the students into teams of two. Darcy wanted to be paired with her close friend, Brisana Meeks. They were both excellent students, a cut above most kids at Bluford, Darcy thought.

"Today, we are forming project teams so that each student can gain something valuable from the other," Ms. Reed said as Darcy sat at her desk. Ms. Reed was a tall, stately woman who reminded Darcy of the Statue of Liberty. She would have been a perfect model for the statue if Lady Liberty had been a black woman. She never would have been called pretty, but it was possible she might have been called a handsome woman. "For this assignment, each of you will be working with someone you've never worked with before."

Darcy was worried. If she was not teamed with Brisana,

maybe she would be teamed with some really dumb student who would pull her down. Darcy was a little ashamed of herself for thinking that way. Grandma used to say that all flowers are equal, but different. The simple daisy was just as lovely as the prize rose. But still Darcy did not want to be paired with some weak partner who would lower her grade.

"Darcy Wills will be teamed with Tarah Carson," Ms. Reed announced.

Darcy gasped. Not Tarah! Not that big, chunky girl with the brassy voice who squeezed herself into tight skirts and wore lime green or hot pink satin tops and cheap jewelry. Not Tarah who hung out with Cooper Hodden, that loser who was barely hanging on to his football eligibility. Darcy had heard that Cooper had been left back once or twice and even got his driver's license as a sophomore. Darcy's face felt hot with anger. Why was Ms. Reed doing this?

Hakeem Randall, a handsome, shy boy who sat in the back row, was teamed with the class blabbermouth, LaShawn Appleby. Darcy had a secret crush on Hakeem since freshman year. So far she had only shared this with her diary, never with another living soul.

It was almost as though Ms. Reed was playing some devilish game. Darcy glanced at Tarah, who was smiling broadly. Tarah had an enormous smile, and her teeth contrasted harshly with her dark red lipstick. "Great," Darcy muttered under her breath.

Ms. Reed ord e red the teams to meet so they could begin to plan their projects.

As she sat down by Tarah, Darcy was instantly sickened by a syrupy-sweet odor.

She must have doused herself with cheap perfume this morning , Darcy thought.

"Hey, girl," Tarah said. "Well, don't you look down in the mouth. What's got you lookin' that way?"

It was hard for Darcy to meet new people, especially someone like Tarah, a person Aunt Charlotte would call "low class." These were people who were loud and rude. They drank too much, used drugs, got into fights and ruined the neighborhood. They yelled ugly insults at people, even at their friends. Darcy did not actually know that Tarah did anything like this personally, but she seemed like the type who did.

"I just didn't think you'd be interested in tidal pools," Darcy explained.

Tarah slammed her big hand on the desk, making her gold bracelets jangle like ice cubes in a glass, and laughed. Darcy had never heard a mule bray, but she was sure it made exactly the same sound. Then Tarah leaned close and whispered, "Girl, I don't know a tidal pool from a fool. Ms. Reed stuck us together to mess with our heads, you hear what I'm sayin'?"

"Maybe we could switch to other partners," Darcy said nervously.

A big smile spread slowly over Tarah's face. "Nah, I think I'm gonna enjoy this. You're always sittin' here like a princess collecting your A's. Now you gotta work with a regular person, so you better loosen up, girl!"

Darcy felt as if her teeth were glued to her tongue. She fumbled in her bag for her outline of the project. It all seemed like a horrible joke now. She and Tarah Carson standing knee-deep in the muck of a tidal pool!

"Worms live there, don't they?" Tarah asked, twisting a big gold ring on her chubby finger.

"Yeah, I guess," Darcy replied.

"Big green worms," Tarah continued. "So if you get your feet stuck in the bottom of that old tidal pool, and you can't get out, do the worms crawl up your clothes?"

Darcy ignored the remark. "I'd like for us to go there soon, you know, look around."

"My boyfriend, Cooper, he goes down to the ocean all the time. He can take us. He says he's seen these fiddler crabs. They look like big spiders, and they'll try to bite your toes off. Cooper says so," Tarah said.

"Stop being silly," Darcy shot back. "If you' re not even going to be serious . . . "

"You think you're better than me, don't you?" Tarah suddenly growled.

"I never said—" Darcy blurted.

"You don't have to say it, girl. It's in your eyes. You think I'm a low-life and you're something special. Well, I got more friends than you got fingers and toes together. You got no friends, and everybody laughs at you behind your back. Know what the word on you is? Darcy Wills give you the chills."

Just then, the bell rang, and Darcy was glad for the excuse to turn away from Tarah, to hide the hot tears welling in her eyes. She quickly rushed from the classroom, relieved that school was over. Darcy did not think she could bear to sit through another class just now.

Darcy headed down the long street towards home. She did not like Tarah . Maybe it was wrong, but it was true. Still, Tarah's brutal words hurt. Even stupid, awful people might tell you the truth about yourself. And Darcy did not have any real friends, except for Brisana. Maybe the other kids were mocking her behind her back. Darcy was very slender, not as shapely as many of the other girls. She remembered the time when Cooper Hodden was hanging in front of the deli with his friends, and he yelled as Darcy went by, "Hey, is that really a female there? Sure don't look like it. Looks more like an old broomstick with hair. " His companions laughed rudely, and Darcy had walked a little faster.

A terrible thought clawed at Darcy. Maybe she was the loser, not Tarah. Tarah was always hanging with a bunch of kids, laughing and joking. She would go down the hall to the lockers and greetings would come from everywhere. "Hey, Tarah!" "What's up, Tar?" "See ya at lunch, girl." When Darcy went to the lockers, there was dead silence.

Darcy usually glanced into stores on her way home from school. She enjoyed looking at the trays of chicken feet and pork ears at the little Asian grocery store. Sometimes she would even steal a glance at the diners sitting by the picture window at the Golden Grill Restaurant. But today she stare d straight ahead, her shoulders drooping.

If this had happened last year, she would have gone directly to Grandma's house, a block from where Darcy lived. How many times had Darcy and Jamee run to Grandma's, eaten applesauce cookies, drunk cider, and poured out their troubles to Grandma. Somehow, their problems would always dissolve in the warmth of her love and wisdom. But now Grandma was a frail figure in the corner of their apartment, saying little. And what little she did say made less and less sense.

Darcy was usually the first one home. The minute she got there, Mom left for the hospital to take the 3:00 to 11:00 shift in the ER. By the time Mom finished her paperwork at the hospital, she would be lucky to be home again by midnight. After Mom left, Darcy went to Grandma's room to give her the malted nutrition drink that the doctor ordered her to have three times a day.

"Want to drink your chocolate malt, Grandma?" Darcy asked, pulling up a chair beside Grandma's bed.

Grandma was sitting up, and her eyes were open. "No. I'm not hungry," she said listlessly. She always said that.

"You need to drink your malt, Grandma," Darcy insisted, gently putting the straw between the pinched lips.

Grandma sucked the malt slowly. "Grandma, nobody likes me at school," Darcy said. She did not expect any response. But there was a strange comfort in telling Grandma anyway. "Everybody laughs at me. It's because I'm shy and maybe stuck-up, too, I guess. But I don't mean to be. Stuck-up, I mean. Maybe I'm weird. I could be weird, I guess. I could be like Aunt Charlotte . . ." Tears rolled down Darcy's cheeks. Her heart ached with loneliness. There was nobody to talk to anymore, nobody who had time to listen, nobody who understood.

Grandma blinked and pushed the straw away. Her eyes brightened as they did now and then. "You are a wonderful girl. Everybody knows that," Grandma said in an almost normal voice. It happened like that sometimes. It was like being in the middle of a dark storm and having the clouds part, revealing a patch of clear, sunlit blue. For just a few precious minutes, Grandma was bright-eyed and saying normal things.

"Oh, Grandma, I'm so lonely," Darcy cried, pressing her head against Grandma's small shoulder.

"You were such a beautiful baby," Grandma said, stroking her hair." 'That one is going to shine like the morning star.' That's what I told your Mama. 'That child is going to shine like the morning star.' Tell me, Angelcake, is your daddy home yet?"

Darcy straightened. "Not yet." Her heart pounded so hard, she could feel it thumping in her chest. Darcy's father had not been home in five years.

"Well, tell him to see me when he gets home. I want him to buy you that blue dress you liked in the store window. That's for you, Angelcake. Tell him I've got money. My social security came, you know. I have money for the blue dress," Grandma said, her eyes slipping shut.

Just then, Darcy heard the apartment door slam. Jamee had come home. Now she stood in the hall, her hands belligerently on her hips. "Are you talking to Grandma again?" Jamee demanded.

"She was talking like normal," Darcy said. "Sometimes she does. You know she does."

"That is so stupid," Jamee snapped. "She never says anything right anymore. Not anything!" Jamee's voice trembled.

Darcy got up quickly and set down the can of malted milk. She ran to Jamee and put her arms around her sister. "Jamee, I know you're hurting too."

"Oh, don't be stupid," Jamee protested, but Darcy hugged her more tightly, and in a few seconds Jamee was crying. "She was the best thing in this stupid house," Jamee cried. "Why'd she have to go?"

"She didn't go," Darcy said. "Not really."

"She did! She did!" Jamee sobbed. She struggled free of Darcy, ran to her room, and slammed the door. In a minute, Darcy heard the bone-rattling sound of rap music.

Lost and Found, *a Bluford Series™ novel, is reprinted with permission from Townsend Press. Copyright © 2002.*

Want to read more? This and other *Bluford Series*™ novels and paperbacks can be purchased for $1 each at www.townsendpress.com.

Teens:
How to Get More Out of This Book

Self-help: The teens who wrote the stories in this book did so because they hope that telling their stories will help readers who are facing similar challenges. They want you to know that you are not alone, and that taking specific steps can help you manage or overcome very difficult situations. They've done their best to be clear about the actions that worked for them so you can see if they'll work for you.

Writing: You can also use the book to improve your writing skills. Each teen in this book wrote 5-10 drafts of his or her story before it was published. If you read the stories closely you'll see that the teens work to include a beginning, a middle, and an end, and good scenes, description, dialogue, and anecdotes (little stories). To improve your writing, take a look at how these writers construct their stories. Try some of their techniques in your own writing.

Reading: Finally, you'll notice that we include the first chapter from a Bluford Series novel in this book, alongside the true stories by teens. We hope you'll like it enough to continue reading. The more you read, the more you'll strengthen your reading skills. Teens at Youth Communication like the Bluford novels because they explore themes similar to those in their own stories. Your school may already have the Bluford books. If not, you can order them online for only $1.

Resources on the Web

We will occasionally post Think About It questions on our website, www.youthcomm.org, to accompany stories in this and other Youth Communication books. We try out the questions with teens and post the ones they like best. Many teens report that writing answers to those questions in a journal is very helpful.

How to Use This Book in Staff Training

Staff say that reading these stories gives them greater insight into what teens are thinking and feeling, and new strategies for working with them. You can help the staff you work with by using these stories as case studies.

Select one story to read in the group, and ask staff to identify and discuss the main issue facing the teen. There may be disagreement about this, based on the background and experience of staff. That is fine. One point of the exercise is that teens have complex lives and needs. Adults can probably be more effective if they don't focus too narrowly and can see several dimensions of their clients.

Ask staff: What issues or feelings does the story provoke in them? What kind of help do they think the teen wants? What interventions are likely to be most promising? Least effective? Why? How would you build trust with the teen writer? How have other adults failed the teen, and how might that affect his or her willingness to accept help? What other resources would be helpful to this teen, such as peer support, a mentor, counseling, family therapy, etc.

Resources on the Web

From time to time we will post Think About It questions on our website, www.youthcomm.org, to accompany stories in this and other Youth Communication books. We try out the questions with teens and post the ones that they find most effective. We'll also post lesson for some of the stories. Adults can use the questions and lessons in workshops.

Teachers and Staff:
How to Use This Book in Groups

When working with teens individually or in groups, using these stories can help young people face difficult issues in a way that feels safe to them. That's because talking about the issues in the stories usually feels safer to teens than talking about those same issues in their own lives. Addressing issues through the stories allows for some personal distance; they hit close to home, but not too close. Talking about them opens up a safe place for reflection. As teens gain confidence talking about the issues in the stories, they usually become more comfortable talking about those issues in their own lives.

Below are general questions that can help you lead discussions about the stories, which help teens and staff reflect on the issues in their own work and lives. In most cases you can read a story and conduct a discussion in one 45-minute session. Teens are usually happy to read the stories aloud, with each teen reading a paragraph or two. (Allow teens to pass if they don't want to read.) It takes 10-15 minutes to read a story straight through. However, it is often more effective to let workshop participants make comments and discuss the story as you go along. The workshop leader may even want to annotate her copy of the story beforehand with key questions.

If teens read the story ahead of time or silently, it's good to break the ice with a few questions that get everyone on the same page: Who is the main character? How old is she? What happened to her? How did she respond? Etc. Another good starting question is: "What stood out for you in the story?" Go around the room and let each person briefly mention one thing.

Then move on to open-ended questions, which encourage participants to think more deeply about what the writers were feeling, the choices they faced, and they actions they took. There are no right or wrong answers to the open-ended questions. Open-ended questions encourage participants to think about how the themes, emotions and choices in the stories relate to their own lives. Here are some examples of open-ended questions that we have found to be effective. You can use variations of these questions with almost any story in this book.

—What main problem or challenge did the writer face?

—What choices did the teen have in trying to deal with the problem?

—Which way of dealing with the problem was most effective for the teen? Why?

—What strengths, skills, or resources did the teen use to address the challenge?

—If you were in the writer's shoes, what would you have done?

—What could adults have done better to help this young person?

—What have you learned by reading this story that you didn't know before?

—What, if anything, will you do differently after reading this story?

—What surprised you in this story?

—Do you have a different view of this issue, or see a different way of dealing with it, after reading this story? Why or why not?

Credits

The stories in this book originally appeared in the following Youth Communication publications:

"Mommy's Baby, Daddy's Maybe," by Anonymous, *Represent*, March/April 2007

"AWOL from Motherhood," by Shannel Walker, *Represent*, March/April 2005

"Weaving Our Own Safety Net," by Fatima Plummer, *Represent*, March/April 2005

"Growing Into Fatherhood," by JulioPagan, *New Youth Connections*, May 1992

"Mom Wasn't Ready for Me," by Anonymous, *Represent*, July/August 2000

"There's More Than One Way to Be a Father," by Frank Marino, *New Youth Connections*, January/February 1994

"I Wish I Had Waited," by Fetima Perkins, *New Youth Connections*, September/October 1999

"Dates with Destiny," by Fetima Perkins, *New Youth Connections*, January/February 1999

"A Day in the Life of a Teen Mom," by Shauntay Jones, *Represent*, May/June 1999

"Staying with the Hurt," by T. Davis, *Represent*, March/April 1994

"A Partner for Parents," by La'Quesha Barner, *Represent*, March/April 2007

"My Teen Body Wasn't Ready for Pregnancy," by Lillian Cremedy, *Represent*, January/February 2001

"It Took Five Tries to Find a Home," by Lillian Cremedy, *Represent*, January/February 2001

"Where the Fathers At?" by Antwaun Garcia, *Represent*, November/December 2001

"Growing Up Together," by Vanessa Sanchez, *Rise*, Summer 2007

"A Mother's Touch," by Natasha Santos, *Represent*, March/April 2007

"Family Man," by Mimi Callaghan, *New Youth Connections*, May/June 1998

"Will I Get My Children Back?" by Jessica DeSince, *Represent*, November/December 1996

"How I Became a Stronger Mother," by Anzula Richardson, *Represent*, November/December 1993

About
Youth Communication

Youth Communication, founded in 1980, is a nonprofit youth development program located in New York City whose mission is to teach writing, journalism, and leadership skills. The teenagers we train become writers for our websites and books and for two print magazines, *New Youth Connections*, a general-interest youth magazine, and *Represent*, a magazine by and for young people in foster care.

Each year, up to 100 young people participate in Youth Communication's school-year and summer journalism workshops where they work under the direction of full-time professional editors. Most are African American, Latino, or Asian, and many are recent immigrants. The opportunity to reach their peers with accurate portrayals of their lives and important self-help information motivates the young writers to create powerful stories.

Our goal is to run a strong youth development program in which teens produce high quality stories that inform and inspire their peers. Doing so requires us to be sensitive to the complicated lives and emotions of the teen participants while also providing an intellectually rigorous experience. We achieve that goal in the writing/teaching/editing relationship, which is the core of our program.

Our teaching and editorial process begins with discussions

between adult editors and the teen staff. In those meetings, the teens and the editors work together to identify the most important issues in the teens' lives and to figure out how those issues can be turned into stories that will resonate with teen readers.

Once story topics are chosen, students begin the process of crafting their stories. For a personal story, that means revisiting events in one's past to understand their significance for the future. For a commentary, it means developing a logical and persuasive point of view. For a reported story, it means gathering information through research and interviews. Students look inward and outward as they try to make sense of their experiences and the world around them and find the points of intersection between personal and social concerns. That process can take a few weeks or a few months. Stories frequently go through ten or more drafts as students work under the guidance of their editors, the way any professional writer does.

Many of the students who walk through our doors have uneven skills, as a result of poor education, living under extremely stressful conditions, or coming from homes where English is a second language. Yet, to complete their stories, students must successfully perform a wide range of activities, including writing and rewriting, reading, discussion, reflection, research, interviewing, and typing. They must work as members of a team and they must accept individual responsibility. They learn to provide constructive criticism, and to accept it. They engage in explorations of truthfulness, fairness, and accuracy. They meet deadlines. They must develop the audacity to believe that they have something important to say and the humility to recognize that saying it well is not a process of instant gratification. Rather, it usually requires a long, hard struggle through many discussions and much rewriting.

It would be impossible to teach these skills and dispositions as separate, disconnected topics, like grammar, ethics, or assertiveness. However, we find that students make rapid progress when they are learning skills in the context of an inquiry that is personally significant to them and that will benefit their peers.

When teens publish their stories—in *New Youth Connections* and *Represent*, on the web, and in other publications—they reach tens of thousands of teen and adult readers. Teachers, counselors, social workers, and other adults circulate the stories to young people in their classes and out-of-school youth programs. Adults tell us that teens in their programs—including many who are ordinarily resistant to reading—clamor for the stories. Teen readers report that the stories give them information they can't get anywhere else, and inspire them to reflect on their lives and open lines of communication with adults.

Writers usually participate in our program for one semester, though some stay much longer. Years later, many of them report that working here was a turning point in their lives—that it helped them acquire the confidence and skills that they needed for success in college and careers. Scores of our graduates have overcome tremendous obstacles to become journalists, writers, and novelists. They include National Book Award finalist Edwidge Danticat, novelist Ernesto Quinonez, writer Veronica Chambers and *New York Times* reporter Rachel Swarns. Hundreds more are working in law, business, and other careers. Many are teachers, principals, and youth workers, and several have started nonprofit youth programs themselves and work as mentors— helping another generation of young people develop their skills and find their voices.

Youth Communication is a nonprofit educational corporation. Contributions are gratefully accepted and are tax deductible to the fullest extent of the law.

To make a contribution, or for information about our publications and programs, including our catalog of over 100 books and curricula for hard-to-reach teens, see www.youthcomm.org

About The Editors

Al Desetta has been an editor of Youth Communication's two teen magazines, *Foster Care Youth United* (now known as *Represent*) and *New Youth Connections*. He was also an instructor in Youth Communication's juvenile prison writing program. In 1991, he became the organization's first director of teacher development, working with high school teachers to help them produce better writers and student publications.

Prior to working at Youth Communication, Desetta directed environmental education projects in New York City public high schools and worked as a reporter.

He has a master's degree in English literature from City College of the City University of New York and a bachelor's degree from the State University of New York at Binghamton, and he was a Revson Fellow at Columbia University for the 1990-91 academic year.

He is the editor of many books, including several other Youth Communication anthologies: *The Heart Knows Something Different: Teenage Voices from the Foster Care System, The Struggle to Be Strong*, and *The Courage to Be Yourself.* He is currently a freelance editor.

Keith Hefner co-founded Youth Communication in 1980 and has directed it ever since. He is the recipient of the Luther P. Jackson Education Award from the New York Association of Black Journalists and a MacArthur Fellowship. He was also a Revson Fellow at Columbia University.

Laura Longhine is the editorial director at Youth Communication. She edited *Represent*, Youth Communication's magazine by and for youth in foster care, for three years, and has written for a variety of publications. She has a BA in English from Tufts University and an MS in Journalism from Columbia University.

More Helpful Books
From Youth Comunication

 *The Struggle to Be Strong: True Stories by Teens About Overcoming Tough Times.* Foreword by Veronica Chambers. Help young people identify and build on their own strengths with 30 personal stories about resiliency. (Free Spirit)

Starting With "I": Personal Stories by Teenagers. "Who am I and who do I want to become?" Thirty-five stories examine this question through the lens of race, ethnicity, gender, sexuality, family, and more. Increase this book's value with the free Teacher's Guide, available from youthcomm.org. (Youth Communication)

 *Real Stories, Real Teens.* Inspire teens to read and recognize their strengths with this collection of 26 true stories by teens. The young writers describe how they overcame significant challenges and stayed true to themselves. Also includes the first chapters from three novels in the Bluford Series. (Youth Communication)

The Courage to Be Yourself: True Stories by Teens About Cliques, Conflicts, and Overcoming Peer Pressure. In 26 first-person stories, teens write about their lives with searing honesty. These stories will inspire young readers to reflect on their own lives, work through their problems, and help them discover who they really are. (Free Spirit)

 *Out With It: Gay and Straight Teens Write About Homosexuality.* Break stereotypes and provide support with this unflinching look at gay life from a teen's perspective. With a focus on urban youth, this book also includes several heterosexual teens' transformative experiences with gay peers. (Youth Communication)

Things Get Hectic: Teens Write About the Violence That Surrounds Them. Violence is commonplace in many teens' lives, be it bullying, gangs, dating, or family relationships. Hear the experiences of victims, perpetrators, and witnesses through more than 50 real-world stories. (Youth Communication)

From Dropout to Achiever: Teens Write About School. Help teens overcome the challenges of graduating, which may involve overcoming family problems, bouncing back from a bad semester, or dropping out for a time. These teens show how they achieve academic success. (Youth Communication)

My Secret Addiction: Teens Write About Cutting. These true accounts of cutting, or self-mutilation, offer a window into the personal and family situations that lead to this secret habit, and show how teens can get the help they need. (Youth Communication)

Sticks and Stones: Teens Write About Bullying. Shed light on bullying, as told from the perspectives of the perpetrator, the victim, and the witness. These stories show why bullying occurs, the harm it causes, and how it might be prevented. (Youth Communication)

Boys to Men: Teens Write About Becoming a Man. The young men in this book write about their confusion, ideals, and the challenges of becoming a man. Their honesty and courage make them role models for teens who are bombarded with contradictory messages about what it means to be a man. (Youth Communication)

Through Thick and Thin: Teens Write About Obesity, Eating Disorders and Self Image. Help teens who struggle with obesity, eating disorders and body weight issues. These stories show the pressures teens face when they are confronted by unrealistic standards for physical appearance, and how emotions can affect the way we eat. (Youth Communication)

To order these and other books, go to:
www.youthcomm.org
or call 212-279-0708 x115